Beyond the Darkness Devotional

BEYOND THE DARKNESS

DEVOTIONAL

40 DAYS OF ENCOURAGEMENT IN GRIEF

CLARISSA MOLL

TYNDALE
MOMENTUM®

A Tyndale nonfiction imprint

Visit Tyndale online at tyndale.com.

Visit Tyndale Momentum online at tyndalemomentum.com.

Tyndale, Tyndale's quill logo, *Tyndale Momentum*, and the Tyndale Momentum logo are registered trademarks of Tyndale House Ministries. Tyndale Momentum is a nonfiction imprint of Tyndale House Publishers, Carol Stream, Illinois.

Beyond the Darkness Devotional: 40 Days of Encouragement in Grief

Designed by Jennifer L. Phelps

Edited by Jonathan Schindler

Published in association with the literary agency of Wolgemuth & Associates.

For information about special discounts for bulk purchases, please contact Tyndale House Publishers at csresponse@tyndale.com, or call 1-855-277-9400.

ISBN 978-1-4964-8756-8

Printed in China

30	29	28	27	26	25	24
7	6	5	4	3	2	1

Contents

Introduction

When will the sadness stop hurting? How will I ever live again? If you've asked these questions after the death of your loved one, you're not alone. Walking through grief can feel like the most isolating and distressing experience you've ever endured. It's normal to long for a life beyond your sadness.

As you walk with sorrow and suffering, Jesus walks beside you too. The prophet Isaiah described him as "a man of sorrows, acquainted with deepest grief" (Isaiah 53:3, NLT). Jesus is the friend who understands. Moreover, Jesus is the one who can impart to you his resurrection life, bringing strength to your weariness and hope to your despair.

From the moment our first parents Adam and Eve fell into sin, all of creation has longed for this resurrection life to be realized. Paul tells the church in Rome that the entire world groans with painful longing as it waits for God's promises to be fulfilled. Hallelujah, Jesus has already come to inaugurate our redemption! And yet, how we long for the brokenness of this world to be repaired, for death's power to be finally stripped away, for all things to be made new. We wait, like Adam and Eve, at the edge of Eden. Some days, resurrection feels a hopeful breath away.

Other days, our grief reveals to us the gulf that stands between where we are and where we long to be.

A forty-day devotional won't fix your grief. Noah grieved for forty days as he watched the world he'd known slip away beneath the floodwaters. Israel grieved for forty years in the desert as they wondered what their future might hold. None of these grief journeys ended when their "forties" were up. Nevertheless, a quiet transformation occurred in every instance. Each person experienced a reorienting, a strengthening, and a sustaining that empowered them to face what God had next for them. I believe the same is possible for you.

As you travel through the Old Testament and dedicate your heart to Scripture over these next forty days, I hope you experience that quiet transformation too. Your loved one's death has thrust you into a sort of exile, a wilderness wandering experience. However, like those ancient Israelites, you do not walk this road alone. Wherever your grief journey takes you, dear friend, you will find God there. May the words in this book remind you of his loving presence and give you courage to live fully again.

Our God is the same

yesterday, today, and forever.

He's not done with this world

or with you, either.

WHERE IT ALL BEGAN

God saw that it was good.

GENESIS 1:10, NIV

On my phone, I keep a picture of my family before death arrived. Taken less than twenty-four hours before my husband Rob's accidental death, the photograph shows our family sitting to watch a tractor pull at the local county fair.

Whenever I look at that picture, I can't help but think of all we didn't know that night. We didn't know that death would come so swiftly. We didn't know we'd never say "I love you" again. We didn't know our children would grow up without a father, an indelible mark imprinted on their lives because of his absence. All we knew was that the elephant ears tasted delicious, the magic show was hokey but entertaining, and the kids doing the tractor pull were surprisingly strong.

You have your own "remember when" stories too. Before the cancer diagnosis. Before the Alzheimer's grew severe. Before the accident, the phone call, the knock at the door. Whether you've lost your person recently or decades ago, looking back on those moments brings pain and an ache that settles deep into your bones. There was a time when life used to be so good.

Unfortunately, pain and hospice, funeral plans and weeping, end-of-life decisions and grief blur our memories. The darkness of loss makes it hard to see God's goodness in our present. So sometimes it helps to first look back before we move forward.

We begin our forty-day journey here—at Creation, where it all began. When God created the world in divine love, he called each thing good—the mountains, the avocados, the flamingos, the swordfish. With gentle care, he crafted man and woman in his image, an intimate reflection of his triune person. Before sin marred God's perfect world, before death came to steal and destroy, life used to be so good—for everyone and everything.

Today, your "remember when" stories may feel like a world away. No doubt, as God looks at his world, he feels the same. Sin has broken everything; death has had its day. Nevertheless, as you travel through this day, hold fast to the hope those happier memories can still offer. Our God is the same yesterday, today, and forever. He's not done with this world or with you, either.

The same tender attention that fashioned the galaxies attends to you today, dear grieving friend. The same strength that hoisted the planets upholds you in your weakness. The same love that created hydrangeas and honeybees still cares about recreating you each morning as you rise. Yes, your life used to be so good; and, by God's amazing power, it can be good again.

I trust in your unfailing love; my heart rejoices in your salvation. I will sing the LORD's praise, for he has been good to me.

PSALM 13:5-6, NIV

Surely your goodness and unfailing love will pursue me all the days of my life.

PSALM 23:6, NLT

A Prayer: God, I know that your goodness follows me all of the days of my life, but I'm struggling to believe that today. My whole life feels like BD/AD—before death and after death. I mark time differently now. More than that, I'm tempted to see my life before loss as good and everything since as bad. As I remember the way life used to be, recall to me your steadfast love. Remind me that your goodness has not ended with my loved one's death. Restore my hope in your promises. Amen.

An Activity for Today: Choose three happy memories of life before your person's death and jot them briefly on the lines below. What made those moments special? How was life good back then? As you reflect on these memories, seek to identify specifically how God's goodness was evident in those circumstances. Did you see God's patience on display? His lavish provision? His abiding love? All these gifts from God then are still available to you now. As you go about your day, be on the lookout for where these gifts might show up for you right where you are today.

_____

_____

_____

_____

_____

_____

_____

A Song to Encourage Your Heart: "Land of the Living (You Don't Lie)" by Church of the City

As we weep in grief

and rail against death's power,

our laments for fairness

rise like prayers

to the heart of God.

IT'S ALL SO UNFAIR

While they were in the field,
Cain attacked his brother Abel and killed him.

GENESIS 4:8, NIV

A brilliant physicist trained at MIT and Harvard, Hans grew old and shaky as grandpas do, but it was the ebbing of his mind that hurt the most to watch. Over the years, dementia stole the man his family knew and loved, leaving him needy, confused, and sometimes very cantankerous. For a man who had survived so much as a child refugee during World War II and accomplished so much (several patents bear his name), this disease that corroded Hans's mind and weakened his body felt supremely unfair.

Alzheimer's is the seventh leading cause of death in the United States, but it's not the only "unfair" way to die. Accidents, cancers, and any number of other causes remind us that, however well we live, our ends may be undignified, harsh, or agonizingly painful. Even for those whose lives end peacefully, there runs an undercurrent of frustration. This life is not as it should be.

No sooner had God created Adam and Eve than grief entered the world's first family. The unfairness of it all strikes us as we read Genesis 4. Young Abel the shepherd faithfully tends his flocks and brings to God the offering he desires. His brother Cain contributes solely to fulfill an obligation. When God determines Abel's offering is acceptable and Cain's isn't, Cain just can't take it. His neck hair bristles, his temperature rises, and in a fit of anger, he lures his brother into a field and kills him. The first murder. The first innocent victim. The first casualty of death's terrible unfairness.

Romans 6 tells us that death is the just payment for our sins. We and our first parents chose to follow our own wisdom instead of God's, and death is the consequence. However, when we grieve our loved one's death saying that life is "unfair," I suspect that our cries of unfairness stem from our deep longing for the final and lasting justice of God. As we weep in grief and rail against death's power, our laments for fairness rise like prayers to the heart of God. Our voices join with the psalmist's when he cries, "How long, O Lord?" (Psalm 13:1).

Today, dear grieving friend, release any inhibitions that might hold you back from telling God how unfair you feel your loss is. Go ahead and express your longing before the Lord. Let him know how wrong everything is, and ask him to make it right. Cry out with grief and desperate hope, "Come quickly, Lord Jesus!"

———

The LORD longs to be gracious to you; therefore he will rise up to show you compassion. For the LORD is a God of justice. Blessed are all who wait for him!
ISAIAH 30:18, NIV

O LORD, come back to us! How long will you delay? Take pity on your servants! Satisfy us each morning with your unfailing love, so we may sing for joy to the end of our lives.
PSALM 90:13-14, NLT

A Prayer: *God, my person's death has revealed to me the great unfairness of this life. I see now in ways I've never seen before how broken we are and how desperately we need your presence. Jesus, in your mercy, return and make all things new! As I wait for the unfair to become fair, for the wrong to be made right, give me patience and strength to face these days. Remind me that you are not slow to keep your promises. Assure me that you walk beside me as I watch and wait for your return. Come quickly, Lord Jesus! Amen.*

An Activity for Today: *Mainstream media and social media often compound our sense of life's unfairness. In grief, we don't need further reinforcement like that. Our hearts are formed by what we dwell upon. Today, as an exercise in self-care and intentional hopefulness, put on your Sherlock Holmes cap and become a good news investigative journalist for the day. Google "good news" and discover media organizations dedicated to reminding us that life is more than destruction and despair. Grab a colleague at the water cooler and ask her what has gone right in her life lately. Text a friend, "Give me some good news!" As you uncover beauty and goodness around you, thank God for these reminders that he has not forgotten his creation.*

A Song to Encourage Your Heart: *"How Long?" by The Porter's Gate*

God reveals to Noah,

and to us,

his solidarity in grief

and strength in loss—

divine shelter in the storm.

SHELTER FROM THE STORM

The LORD regretted that he had made man on the earth,
and it grieved him to his heart.

GENESIS 6:6, ESV

Do you remember the moment when you realized you'd found your first best friend? The boy who sat across from you at lunch collected baseball cards just like you did. The group of girls who played on the monkey bars at recess invited you to hang upside down with them. Your quiet lab partner in college casually dropped a song lyric over a dissection project, and you knew you'd found a connection.

We rejoice to discover friends who think like us and enjoy the same things we do. These relationships, rooted in common interests and values, sustain us through life's shifts. Many of us struggle after the death of a loved one to maintain these connections, however. Loss creates a divide that many relationships can't seem to span. Friends who were close may fade with time, and we're left wondering if anybody understands what it's like to live with grief like we do. We long for deep understanding, unconditional solidarity, and compassionate care.

What a surprising comfort we find in Genesis 6 as we see God survey the world he has made. Following their own desires, God's beloved creations say to their Maker in word and deed, "You're not my best friend anymore." These creatures God

BEYOND THE DARKNESS DEVOTIONAL

formed in love have rejected him, and his heart tears in two. God grieves. If you've wondered if you could find a friend who understands your sadness in all of its complexity, including the strained relationships after loss, you find him here.

Genesis 6 offers even more comfort, though. God enjoys companionship with Noah, a righteous man whose heart is aligned with his, and God preserves that friendship. Safe in an ark for forty days and forty nights, Noah floats above death and destruction toward a new life. God hides him away and protects him. God reveals to Noah, and to us, his solidarity in grief and strength in loss—divine shelter in the storm.

In the same way, God invites us into the shelter of his presence. Like that floating boat, God is our ark. He preserves us so that the sorrows of life don't wash us away. Today, hurry to God, your ark. Find refuge in his love and comfort in knowing that he truly understands.

⎯⎯

The LORD is close to the brokenhearted; he rescues those whose spirits are crushed.
PSALM 34:18, NLT

God is our refuge and strength, an ever-present help in trouble. Therefore we will not fear, though the earth give way and the mountains fall into the heart of the sea, though its waters roar and foam and the mountains quake with their surging.
PSALM 46:1-3, NIV

A Prayer: Heavenly Father, my friendships have always brought me solace, but in my grief I need something more today. I grieve the friends who have left me alone in my loss. I grieve the relationships that used to bring me joy. I take comfort that you understand and grieve beside me. Remind me this day to seek shelter in your love. Hide me in Jesus. Enclose me in your care and preserve me so that grief doesn't overwhelm me. I trust in you, my God. Amen.

An Activity for Today: When friendships feel thin, it can be helpful to count our blessings. On the lines below make a list of the friends who have stuck beside you since your person died. Add to your list new relationships that have been born from your grief—whether it's a person at your church who has also experienced loss, a friendly hospice nurse who served your family, or your electrician who said he'd do the job for free when he heard you were grieving.

Take a moment to thank God for these people in your life who know your sorrows and stand with you in them. Then take it a step further. Text two or three of the folks on your list and let them know you love them. God has placed each of these people in your life as tangible reminders of his presence with you. Thank these friends for being the hands and feet of Jesus!

_____

_____

_____

_____

A Song to Encourage Your Heart: "Jesus Lover of My Soul" by Tasha Cobbs Leonard (featuring The Walls Group)

Though death creates a new
landscape in our lives, God
knows the topography already.
He will guide us through it
toward abundant life again.

DIRECTIONS, PLEASE?

*"Go from your country, your people and your
father's household to the land I will show you."* . . .
So Abram went, as the LORD had told him.

GENESIS 12:1, 4, NIV

In 1804, Meriweather Lewis and William Clark set out from St.
Louis, Missouri, to find a new way through the west. Over the
next two years, Lewis and Clark traveled approximately eight
thousand miles—much of it through territory that had never
been mapped.

In a world where we enjoy GPS and sports apps that map
out our runs, it's mind boggling to imagine what those years
of navigation looked like for Lewis and Clark. As the men and
their Corps of Discovery set out, they didn't really know what
lay ahead. No doubt, there were moments on their journey when
they wished they could ask for directions.

The death of a loved one drops us into similarly unknown
territory without a map. Even if you've lost other friends or
family before, each particular loss requires that you relearn the
topography of grief. Supporters might encourage you to follow
a linear path through five stages of grief, but you quickly see the
journey will be far more complex. Like Lewis and Clark, you will
need to chart your own course.

As Christians, we are a wandering people, longing for a

better country. Especially after the death of a loved one, this identity grows clear in our mind's eye. This world is not our home. And yet it is. God has placed us here and now to love and serve him. He calls us to follow him, even when we don't know where we are going. As he did for Abram, God assures us, "I will show you where to go." These words are the breadcrumb trail that will lead us forward when we can't orient ourselves in our sorrow. Though death creates a new landscape in our lives, God knows the topography already. He will guide us through it toward abundant life again.

Someday your travels with grief will be well trod. The landscape that now feels so daunting will become mapped as you walk with Jesus through it. Most amazing of all, your journey may one day provide encouragement to another person new to the path—comfort with the comfort you've received. No footfall will be lost. No mile will be wasted. Today, as you walk with God through your loss, take heart. God's got the directions. He will guide your feet in wisdom and love.

———

Whether you turn to the right or to the left, your ears will hear a voice behind you, saying, "This is the way; walk in it."
ISAIAH 30:21, NIV

Show me your ways, LORD, teach me your paths. Guide me in your truth and teach me, for you are God my Savior, and my hope is in you all day long.
PSALM 25:4-5, NIV

A Prayer: *God, I stand with Abram at the edge of a new life, and I don't know where I'm going. The unknown makes me afraid, uneasy, and frustrated. I used to have a life whose contours I knew. I miss its old, familiar landscape. Still, I know that you know the way that I take. You have designed my path in love, and you will lead me every step of the way. As I move about this day, remind me that you are guiding me. Assure me that you have mapped my life and I can trust your direction. Give me faith to step out today and follow you. Amen.*

An Activity for Today: *Rain or shine, step outside your home or work and take a short walk today. Choose a familiar route or map out a new one; it matters less where you go than that you do it! As you walk, pay attention to your body. Feel the swing of your arms at your sides. Press your feet into the ground and sense your stride. Breathe deeply of the air around you and turn your face to the sky. While you engage your whole body in your walk, imagine Jesus walking beside you—not in front, not behind, but right next to you. If prayer comes naturally, talk to Jesus. If worship bubbles up, hum a tune. Or if imagining Jesus' presence is* **tough** *for you right now, simply walk in silence. Even in the quiet,* **you** *are not abandoned; you are beloved.*

A Song to Encourage Your Heart: *"Just a Closer Walk with Thee" by Patsy Cline*

God understands Sarah's

heart, and he responds with

audacious confidence. He sees

a world beyond what Sarah

can even imagine.

DON'T MAKE ME LAUGH

*The LORD said to Abraham, "Why did Sarah laugh
and say, 'Will I really have a child, now that I am
old?' Is anything too hard for the LORD?"*

GENESIS 18:13-14, NIV

"Make 'em laugh, make 'em laugh," sings Donald O'Connor
in the classic musical *Singin' in the Rain*. He romps across sofas,
slams into faux brick walls, and dances with the antics of a circus
performer. "Don't you know everyone wants to laugh?"

Even if O'Connor is right that we want to laugh, most of
us believe there's an appropriate and an inappropriate time to
let out a guffaw. We consider laughter to be something that we
do only when we're already happy. Laughing in the face of loss,
suffering, and tragedy is just wrong. Or is it?

Genesis 18 tells us that Sarah laughs when she hears the
divine messenger's promise of a child. It's a laugh of wry wist-
fulness. A sarcastic chuckle. Sarah doesn't believe there could
be something more to her life than sadness. Loss has narrowed
her vision. Barrenness, miscarriage, and infertility have told her
a single narrative that has come to define her. All she can and
should expect is a life of lack. God's goodness has passed her by.

You may feel like God's goodness has passed you by too.
If you laugh at all anymore, it's a Sarah kind of laugh, full of
heartache. You grieve with her for the happiness that could

have been and for the joys that will never be. You can't imagine a life where laughter could bubble up without sorrow drowning it out.

God understands Sarah's heart, and he responds with audacious confidence. He sees a world beyond what Sarah can even imagine. "Is anything too hard for the LORD?" God asks, knowing, of course, that a baby is precisely the gift Sarah considers impossible to receive. In that tender yet firm reply, God transforms Sarah's laughter into something more than a disappointed chuckle. Sarah's laugh becomes the foretaste of joy that awaits as she trusts in God, her first faltering act of faith.

British playwright Christopher Fry once said, "Comedy is an escape, not from truth but from despair: a narrow escape into faith." Today, as you walk with God, invite him to break open your heart in this kind of laughter. When you can't imagine a life beyond your grief, ask God to unveil your eyes to see his goodness. He can bring joy to your lips again.

———

You have turned my mourning into joyful dancing. You have taken away my clothes of mourning and clothed me with joy, that I might sing praises to you and not be silent. O LORD my God, I will give you thanks forever!
PSALM 30:11-12, NLT

He will once again fill your mouth with laughter and your lips with shouts of joy.
JOB 8:21, NLT

A Prayer: *God, it's been a long time since I've really laughed. It feels as though death has sucked all the joy out of my life. When I hear your promises, like Sarah, I sometimes sarcastically chuckle in disbelief too. In this season, I find it hard to believe that your goodness will follow me all the days of my life. Nevertheless, I know that you are a good God who is faithful in lovingkindness. Give me new eyes to see your work and renew my heart to trust your promises. Help me today to laugh as an act of faith. Amen.*

An Activity for Today: *"Laughter has quantifiable positive physiologic benefits,"* write researchers Louie, Brook, and Frates.[1] *Laughter improves mood, lowers blood pressure, and reduces stress. Best of all, you don't need to have something genuinely hilarious to start a laugh that offers those benefits!*

Today, laugh for your health. Google knock-knock jokes and read them aloud. Allow yourself to smile at their entry-level humor. Watch a funny movie or TV show with a friend—one that's guaranteed to make you chuckle even if it's through tears. Let your friend's laughter become contagious and infect you. Finally, if all else fails, fake it. That's right! Researchers at Georgia State University found that *"playful simulated laughter"* (the physiological act of laughing) had health benefits even when no humor was attached to the event.[2] Sit and giggle for two to four minutes and let laughter bring you hope.

A Song to Encourage Your Heart: *"Mourning into Dancing"* by Steve Green

Though others forsake her,

Hagar knows without a doubt

that God is never blind to her

plight. God notices.

DO YOU SEE ME?

She gave this name to the LORD who spoke to her:
"You are the God who sees me," for she said,
"I have now seen the One who sees me."

GENESIS 16:13, NIV

Few of us actually know what it is like to live without physical eyesight. But after the loss of a loved one, you may wonder if those around you have been afflicted with "blindness." You grieve and feel unseen. You struggle to adjust to life without your person and feel unnoticed. You begin to wonder if anybody cares at all, if your sorrows have enveloped you in a dark cloud of sadness that nobody can see through.

Sarah's servant Hagar knew what it felt to live unseen like that. Hagar lived in submission to a woman who mistreated her and seethed with jealousy at her fertility. Though Abraham and Sarah had received God's promise of a son, they took matters into their own hands, forcing Hagar to conceive and bear Abraham's heir when God didn't meet their timing expectations. But when Hagar became pregnant, Sarah angrily banished her to the desert. Hagar was marginalized, abused, and left all alone. It was as though she were invisible.

As she waited by a desert oasis, Hagar received a life-changing visit. An angel of the Lord appeared to her and instructed her what to do next. When she despaired of life, Hagar discovered for the first time that she wasn't as invisible as she'd always felt. There was a God who saw her.

Hagar goes down in biblical history as the first person to ever give God a special name—El Roi, "the God who sees." And being seen by God changes everything for her. Eventually, her life includes more pain. She ends up back in the desert a second time, this time with her young son. Again, God sees her need, visits her, and sustains her. Her life of sorrow is marked by the most powerful comfort of all. Though others forsake her, Hagar knows without a doubt that God is never blind to her plight. God notices.

Are you feeling invisible today? Do you feel like those around you are blind, that they can't see how much you're struggling and need care? Turn to El Roi today for comfort and provision. The same God that met Hagar in her life's desert will meet you in yours. You are seen, known, and loved beyond measure.

———

Can a mother forget the baby at her breast and have no compassion on the child she has borne? Though she may forget, I will not forget you!
ISAIAH 49:15, NIV

Though the LORD is exalted, he looks kindly on the lowly; though lofty, he sees them from afar. Though I walk in the midst of trouble, you preserve my life.
PSALM 138:6-7, NIV

A Prayer: *Lord, I feel forgotten. Grief clouds my vision, and I fear that it makes me invisible to others too. I long to be really, truly seen. Come to my aid today, just as you did for Hagar in the desert. Notice me and have mercy on me in my loneliness. Instruct me in the way I should go, and give me confidence that you pay attention to each step I take. You see me because you made me and you love me. Remind me that you notice every small detail of my life. Amen.*

An Activity for Today: *God gave us five senses to enjoy our world, but limiting one sense can often heighten the others. Take a few minutes today to sit in silence with your eyes closed. As you "shut off" your vision for the moment, place a hand gently over your heart and still your body. Notice your breathing and the way your body settles as you relax into the moment. Next, attune yourself to your other senses. Is there a lingering taste on your tongue? What do you smell? What can you hear? What do you touch? Exercise these other senses by identifying three things you can taste, smell, hear, or touch. This practice of mindfulness relaxes your body and allows your mind to rest as well.*

A Song to Encourage Your Heart: *"The God Who Sees" by Kathie Lee Gifford and Nicole C. Mullen*

God has asked you to walk by faith and not by sight. How can you walk this hard road of obedience? The same way Abraham did—one small step at a time.

THE GREATEST SACRIFICE

*Abraham answered, "God himself will provide
the lamb for the burnt offering, my son." And
the two of them went on together.*

GENESIS 22:8, NIV

After years of praying for a child, Abraham finally had the son
for which he'd always longed. Isaac, the child whose name meant
"laughter," brought so much joy to his father's heart. From his
first gurgles and coos, Isaac confirmed God's promise to listen
and act on his people's behalf.

Then Abraham received another call to go where he was
told. This one was so different, so dark, so heartbreaking. This
time, God wasn't asking Abraham to let go of his familiar sur-
roundings, his group of friends, or his homeland. He was asking
Abraham to lay his own heart on the altar, to give up the boy he
loved best of all.

How could Abraham do this? Genesis 22 tells us that
Abraham trusted God one small step at a time. He got up in
the morning. He saddled his donkey. He cut wood. He walked
along the road. He did the small things that needed to be done,
trusting that the one who had led him thus far would lead him
through this most challenging act of faith.

Just like Abraham, God has called you to a difficult task—
to live and grow with grief. God has asked you to trust his

mysterious wisdom and plan, to walk by faith and not by sight through the darkest valley of the shadow of death. How can you walk this hard road of obedience? The same way Abraham did— one small step at a time.

Today, as you grieve your loss, take it slow. Get out of bed. Dress for work. Unload the dishwasher. Take a shower. Whatever simple task you can complete, do it with the energy God gives. Each of these seemingly small tasks becomes an act of trust when offered to God. While you go about the mundane routines of your day, remember Abraham's words: "God will provide a lamb." God will honor your fragile obedience, your timid faith. He will give you all that you need. He will lead you in perfect love toward life, one small step at a time.

He who did not spare his own Son, but gave him up for us all— how will he not also, along with him, graciously give us all things?
ROMANS 8:32, NIV

My God will supply every need of yours according to his riches in glory in Christ Jesus.
PHILIPPIANS 4:19, ESV

A Prayer: *Heavenly Father, I'm not sure how to keep going each day. I'm tired from the tasks of grief. I'm weary from the emotions of my loss. Like Abraham, I don't know what you're doing or why. I wish this road of sorrow wasn't so hard. But I trust that you know what it means to watch a loved one die. You understand my grief, not only as a companion but as my God, my guide, and the lifter of my head. Give me the strength to meet this day and all it holds. Empower me to step forward in faith and do the things that need to be done. I choose to trust your wisdom, even when I cannot understand your plan. Amen.*

An Activity for Today: *Whether you're dealing with brain fog from grief or you're overwhelmed with the tasks before you, today engage in list making to help order your next steps. On the lines below, write out self-care tasks that need to be completed. Tasks might include showering, brushing your teeth, getting a haircut, or painting your nails. Next, choose three that you'll complete today. Your body needs to be your first priority in grief. Enlist a friend if you need help getting these items done. You can tackle other hard assignments another day. For today, be like Abraham and get up, saddle your donkey, and cut your wood.*

_____

_____

_____

_____

_____

A Song to Encourage Your Heart: *"Holy Is the Lord" by Andrew Peterson*

God meets you in your

weakness with his power and

strength. He understands

that you are dust, and he will

breathe life into you again

as the days go by.

NEVER-ENDING SADNESS

*All his sons and daughters came to comfort
him, but he refused to be comforted.*

GENESIS 37:35, NIV

The night we received word that my husband had died, I entered
a season of shock. Even though I believed the news, the thought
that my dear husband had fallen to his death on our family vaca-
tion defied all logic. These things weren't supposed to happen!
This couldn't be true!

This kind of disorientation is common after loss. So when
you read the story of Joseph's capture in Genesis 37, you understand his father Jacob's sorrow. Joseph, that cocky favored son,
had shared his grandiose dreams with his brothers, much to
their dislike. His brothers fomented a plot, and Joseph ended
up carted away into slavery in Egypt, all while his father Jacob
believed his favorite son had died in the grip of a wild beast.
How could such a terrible thing happen?

Genesis 37 tells us that Jacob was undone when he learned of
his son's supposed death. He tore his clothes, dressed in mourning garb, and grieved for days on end. Such intense sorrow, no
doubt, came along with all the physical manifestations of shock
we now know attend such traumatic news. We can imagine Jacob
wandering aimlessly, expecting Joseph's voice, losing sleep, and
crying until his body was exhausted.

In this shock, he refused comfort. His sons and daughters could not offer words of solace. Nothing could ease the crushing pain of unexpectedly losing the child he loved. "I will go to my grave mourning for my son," Jacob said (Genesis 37:35, NLT), and he really meant it. Grief would follow him all the days of his life.

Whether your loved one's death came by surprise or with warning, shock and acute distress are normal after loss. Disbelief can linger for months, and even the best attempts at comfort can feel totally inadequate. Jacob's response to news of his son's death isn't overly dramatic; it's natural and appropriate. Moreover, his response isn't a display of weak faith. Yours isn't either.

If you're experiencing severe grief today, don't feel like you need to stuff it down or run away from it. You can grieve deeply and fully, just like Jacob. As you do, turn to your sorrows with compassion. Offer yourself extra gentle care. God meets you in your weakness with his power and strength. He understands that you are dust, and he will breathe life into you again as the days go by. What you've experienced is earth shattering. It's okay if your body, mind, and heart are struggling to take it all in.

———

The LORD is near to the brokenhearted and saves the crushed in spirit.

PSALM 34:18, ESV

LORD, you are the God who saves me; day and night I cry out to you. May my prayer come before you; turn your ear to my cry. I am overwhelmed with troubles and my life draws near to death. I am counted among those who go down to the pit; I am like one without strength.

PSALM 88:1-4, NIV

A Prayer: *God, I can't believe this has happened to me. I can't believe all of the ways my person's absence is going to affect my life. It feels like too much to take in right now. Some days I think I can make it, and other days seem impossible. I don't think anything can really comfort me the way I need. Still, I believe that your Holy Spirit is the Comforter, a gift to me through faith in Jesus. As I wrestle with the reality of my loss, give me relief, support, and solace through your Spirit. Thank you for bearing this burden with and for me. Amen.*

An Activity for Today: *Assemble a simple comfort kit to access when you need care on the go. Grab a Ziploc bag, makeup bag, or grocery bag and fill it with a few items that bring you comfort. A small package of tissues, a tea bag of your favorite flavor, a peppermint or candy, a picture of you with your person, a note card with a Bible verse written on it, a small bottle of scented essential oil—whatever offers you relaxation or a sense of peacefulness. Place your comfort kit in your workbag or purse so that it is nearby if you need it when you're out and about.*

A Song to Encourage Your Heart: *"Help My Unbelief" by Red Mountain Music*

Every successive loss is a

chance to become bitter or

to become better—a chance

to harden to the world's pain

or soften as God nurtures the

fruits of the Spirit within you.

WHAT NEXT?

Moses was afraid, thinking, "Everyone knows what I did." And sure enough, Pharaoh heard what had happened, and he tried to kill Moses. But Moses fled from Pharaoh and went to live in the land of Midian.

EXODUS 2:14-15, NLT

The book of Exodus tells the story of Moses, a man whose life was marked by an avalanche of losses. Threatened by Pharaoh's order to kill all the Israelite baby boys, Moses' mother placed her newborn in a basket in the bulrushes along a river's edge. To her relief and grief, her baby was discovered and adopted into the home of Pharaoh's daughter. Before he could walk or talk, Moses had lost his biological family.

Years later, in early manhood, Moses wrestled with the loss of his identity; he was a Hebrew by blood but an Egyptian by position. Where did he belong? His frustration born of these losses drove him to kill a man in anger, an act that required him to flee into the wilderness. He'd lost his family, his identity, his home. Now he'd lost his safety. Each loss seemed to beget another one.

However, in the vulnerability of that desert, Moses made a startling discovery. God could fill Moses' losses with his presence. As he commissioned Moses to lead the Israelites out of bondage, God would show Moses over and over that each loss invited a choice: Would grief harden his heart or break it open? Each plague that befell Egypt invited that choice. Each subsequent struggle in the desert would too. In the face of one loss after another, Moses would always need to decide—*Will I follow God more nearly or determine my own path through suffering?*

Chances are, the death of your person has precipitated an avalanche of its own. One loss sent you reeling, but you're quickly discovering more losses keep coming. Maybe you've lost your energy and enthusiasm for work. Or you've lost your physical health. Friendships or family relationships may have become strained in the wake of your person's death. Like an avalanche that keeps rolling down the mountain, building speed as it goes, your person's death has created a vast, complicated landscape of devastating loss. You've got so many secondary losses that you feel like you're up to your neck in the snows of grief.

The avalanche of losses in your life offers you the same opportunity it did Moses. Every successive loss is a chance to become bitter or to become better—a chance to harden in response to the world's pain or soften as God nurtures the fruits of the Spirit within you. Will your loved one's death prompt you to turn to the Lord? You bear the burden of so many losses—the immediate and the secondary. Today, allow those griefs to drive you to your heavenly Father.

The waves of death overwhelmed me; floods of destruction swept over me. The grave wrapped its ropes around me; death laid a trap in my path. But in my distress I cried out to the LORD; yes, I cried to my God for help. He heard me from his sanctuary; my cry reached his ears.
2 SAMUEL 22:5-7, NLT

When you go through deep waters, I will be with you. When you go through rivers of difficulty, you will not drown.
ISAIAH 43:2, NLT

A Prayer: God, I lost my person, and now I'm losing other things—friends, health, energy, hope. I am overwhelmed by the many ways my person's death has covered my life in sadness. I feel inundated by loss. I know these griefs bear the temptation to turn from you, but I don't want to do that. Let each successive loss drive me closer to you. Protect me from bitterness and cynicism. Lead me away from the temptations of fatalistic thinking and despair. Restore hope within me as I do the hard work of shoveling through these losses. Remind me that you are with me, working beside me even when I can't see it. Amen.

An Activity for Today: From infancy, we've had places that have brought us comfort. In the boxes below, identify three places that signify peace, joy, and relaxation to you. Next, sit in silence and spend time visualizing one of these locations. What do you see, smell, and hear? Imagine yourself in the mental picture, both as an observer and as a participant. How does it feel when the sand slips between your toes or the wind blows in your hair? Let the location help you relax as you enter mentally and emotionally into it.

A Song to Encourage Your Heart: "God I Look to You" by Bethel Music

When the Israelites can only see death on every side, God makes a way to life again. God parts the waters for Israel's rescue, and he'll do the same for you.

AT THE WATER'S EDGE

I will sing to the LORD, for he is highly exalted.
Both horse and driver he has hurled into the sea.

EXODUS 15:1, NIV

As the fourth anniversary of my husband's death approached, I rented canoes for an overnight family trip to honor his love for the outdoors and connect as we remembered his death.

In a perfect summer season, my idea would have worked beautifully, but this particular summer brought heavy rains that caused the river to rise to dangerous levels. A few days before we were ready to set off, I received an email from the rental company. "High river warning," the subject line read. My heart sank. I knew we'd need to reschedule. Water is powerful; sometimes there's just no way to beat it.

As the Israelites stood on the banks of the Red Sea, their hearts must have sunk too. God had miraculously orchestrated their escape from Pharaoh's enslavement, and they were free. But also *not* free. Hemmed between Pharaoh's approaching armies and water they could not cross, they sensed fear, disillusionment, panic, and frustration well up within them like a summer river rising. How could God lead them this far only to abandon them at the water's edge? Drowning or death at the hands of the Egyptians appeared to be the only two options.

The death of a loved one can often lead us toward this kind

of binary thinking. Loss floods us with emotion and changes the landscape of our lives, and we feel stuck, just like the Israelites. As we look at the Red Sea of grief before us, we're pretty sure we can't go on, but we know we can't go home, either. The past is closed forever to us, and our futures look bleak. We see no way out.

In this place of grief and desperation, God comes to us just as he did to the Israelites that day by the Red Sea. God responds to their and our frustration and fear with amazing kindness. When the Israelites can only see death on every side, God makes a way to life again. God parts the waters for Israel's rescue, and he'll do the same for you.

Where are the floodwaters rising in your life today? Where do riptides of grief or undertows of anger threaten to sweep you off your feet? Where do you need rescue today? God stands waiting with a mighty arm to save you. He is ready to remind you that more than death, suffering, and trials surround you. Today, don't believe the lie that loss is all there is left for you. God will make a way through your own Red Sea and bring you to shores of rest.

———

Let your unfailing love surround us, LORD, for our hope is in you alone.

PSALM 33:22, NLT

Don't let the floods overwhelm me, or the deep waters swallow me, or the pit of death devour me. Answer my prayers, O LORD, for your unfailing love is wonderful. Take care of me, for your mercy is so plentiful.

PSALM 69:15-16, NLT

A Prayer: *Almighty God, the waters of grief rise around me. The power of death's current threatens to sweep me away. I am engulfed by sorrow, and I don't see a way out. Save me from drowning in despair, and set me on firm ground again. I trust that you will open up a way for me just as you did for Israel by the Red Sea. You preserve those you love, and I believe that you will take care of me. Amen.*

An Activity for Today: *Everybody needs a hug sometimes. In fact, researchers have found that even a self-hug can reduce cortisol, the hormone produced by our brains in distress.[3] Today, determine that you will give yourself at least three hugs during the day. To give yourself a hug that really affects your neurobiology, cross your arms across your chest and place your palms on your upper arms. Take a deep breath in, raise your shoulders, and gently squeeze and hold, just like you were hugging a friend. If it feels good, gently rub your palms on your upper arms as you hug yourself. As you self-hug, envision the arms of God enfolding you. You are held by a good, strong God who has engraved your name on the palms of his hands.*

A Song to Encourage Your Heart: *"Red Sea Road" by Ellie Holcomb*

Though the Israelites would doubt his promises and look to satisfy their desires elsewhere, God showed up with dinner every day. In doing so, he gave his people himself—the only food that would ever satisfy.

FOOD FOR THE HUNGRY

The people of Israel ate manna for forty years until
they arrived at the land where they would settle.

EXODUS 16:35, NLT

USDA research tells us that thirty-four million Americans—folks living in our own neighborhoods—frequently go to bed hungry.[4] In a country with over sixty thousand grocery stores and a Starbucks on every corner, that reality boggles the mind. While we may not personally know deep hunger, it's inevitable that we rub shoulders every day with some who do.

The death of your loved one has brought another kind of hunger into your life—an emptiness that nags like a growling belly. You wake up in the morning, and the day that stands before you feels empty without your person. The calendar on the wall documents all the plans you've had to cancel since your person died. An empty schedule, an empty life where there used to be activity and joy.

Just one month after God parted the Red Sea and rescued the nation from slavery, the Israelites' stomachs began to grumble. Gone were the food caches they'd brought from Egypt. They'd gobbled those up right away. Doubt began to gnaw. "We sat around pots filled with meat and ate all the bread we wanted," the Israelites reminisced about their years under Pharaoh's thumb (Exodus 16:3, NLT). Rose-colored glasses distorted their memories of the past. Anything would look tasty at this point—even slavery.

If you have experienced the natural emptiness that comes with grief, you know this temptation. Death eats a hole in your life, in your plans for the future, and it's easy to imagine a quick fix that could make the ache go away. Many bereaved people find that temptations like eating for comfort, using alcohol or drugs, or carelessly pursuing new relationships rise up to allure in ways they never did before. Lack entices us to grasp for sustenance in any place we can find it, even when we know the false promises of worldly pleasure.

God provided food for the Israelites in response to their grumbling. Every morning, like an Uber Eats delivery, fresh manna arrived at their doorsteps. For the next forty years, God never provided a subpar meal. Though the Israelites would doubt his promises and look to satisfy their desires elsewhere, God showed up with dinner every day. In doing so, he gave his people himself—the only food that would ever satisfy.

As you wrestle with your emptiness, are you facing temptations today? Offer God your hungriness, and ask him to fill it with good things cooked up just for you. Resist the urge to seek satisfaction apart from his provision. God promises to nourish you with his presence and provide for every need you have.

The eyes of all look to you, and you give them their food in due season. You open your hand; you satisfy the desire of every living thing.
PSALM 145:15-16, ESV

As the living Father sent me, and I live because of the Father, so whoever feeds on me, he also will live because of me.
JOHN 6:57, ESV

A Prayer: God, my person's death has left me feeling empty. I hunger for relationships, for energy, for hope, for purpose. It feels like I've lost so much. I confess that my emptiness makes me long for easy satisfaction. I crave the "fast food" pleasures of life that give me a false boost of happiness. Draw near to me and keep me from sin. Help me to resist the temptations all around me. Give me your Holy Spirit as Counselor and Guide, directing me ever toward your promises of true nourishment and abundant life. Amen.

An Activity for Today: Food offers us powerful connections to memory. Today, think of a food that reminds you of your person. Did you have a favorite restaurant you frequented together? Order takeout today in his memory. Does a decaf mocha latte she always ordered at Starbucks or the mashed potatoes he requested every Thanksgiving bring your person back to you? Run through the drive-through window on your way to work, or ask a friend to pick up a sack of potatoes for you when she goes for her grocery run. Connect with your person through the smells and tastes of a special food and remember that God provides everything you need, from the calories you require to keep going to the sweet memories of the person you have loved and lost.

A Song to Encourage Your Heart: "Provision" by Mike Janzen

God's call to honest, faithful

worship orients us toward

the one Source that will tell

the truest story of who and

whose we are.

HOMEMADE GODS

*All the people took off their earrings and brought them to
Aaron. He took what they handed him and made it into an
idol cast in the shape of a calf, fashioning it with a tool.*

EXODUS 32:3-4, NIV

Have you ever heard a "big fish" story—where a fisherman's prize
catch grows with each retelling of the story until it's the size of
Moby Dick? If we're honest, we're all prone to exaggeration of
that sort. We overestimate our abilities. We add drama to our
stories. Our worries grow big and take on a life of their own.

The Israelites struggled with the same habit, especially as
they grieved Moses' departure up Mount Sinai to receive God's
law. Without him around, their doubts about God's faithfulness
began to grow. In response, Moses' brother Aaron offered his
own practical solution: idolize the ordinary when you struggle to
fix your gaze on the extraordinary.

Inevitably, we, too, have created idols in our grief. Whether
we've idolized our person or idolized the past, we've all been
guilty of melting down the life we had and refashioning it into
a story that we thought could take away the sadness. Like a big
fish story gone awry, we've convinced ourselves at one time or
another that the past was bigger and better. Instead of sitting
with our sadness, we've tried to fix it by creating something
larger than life.

As we grieve with honesty, God calls us to leave our home-made gods behind. He asks us to reject blind worship of the past. He invites us to see the people and events of our lives for what they truly are. God commands us to worship him alone, not any lifestyle we've lost or person we miss or future we'd hoped to secure. Admittedly, it's a tough request when we're grieving; but God's call to honest, faithful worship orients us toward the one Source that will tell the truest story of who and whose we are.

Today, as you remember your person, be honest about his or her failures or successes. Don't lionize or demonize. Resist the temptation to create idols that replace God at the center of your heart. Your grief offers the opportunity to recommit yourself to following God alone.

Do not put your trust in princes, in human beings, who cannot save. When their spirit departs, they return to the ground; on that very day their plans come to nothing. Blessed are those whose help is the God of Jacob, whose hope is in the LORD their God.
PSALM 146:3-5, NIV

And now here's what I want you to do: Tell the truth, the whole truth, when you speak. Do the right thing by one another, both personally and in your courts. Don't cook up plans to take unfair advantage of others. Don't do or say what isn't so. I hate all that stuff. Keep your lives simple and honest.
ZECHARIAH 8:16-17, MSG

A Prayer: *Dear Jesus, when I think about life before my loss, I confess that I tend to tell myself an edited story of the past. I create little idols in my life to fill the space that grief has made. However, I know that these attempts will never bring true solace to my heart. Only your truth can set my spirit free to live fully again. Forgive me. As I remember my person, help me to be honest. As I grieve, keep me from shaping false gods. Enliven me to worship you alone. Amen.*

An Activity for Today: *Acknowledging mortality and finitude is an ongoing exercise in grief work. Today, if you are able, visit the cemetery where your person is buried. Simply sit in your car or beside the grave and practice rest. If you are unable to visit the cemetery because of distance or other complexity, take a moment and fill in the stone on this page. After listing your person's name and dates of birth and death, what would you add if you were asked to design it—a picture, a lyric from a song, a Bible verse? Draw this imaginary stone for your person, thanking God for their life and entrusting them to him in death.*

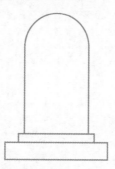

A *Song* to Encourage Your Heart: *"I Glory in Christ" by Sandra McCracken*

This landscape of loss that

feels so foreboding is infused

with divine Presence.

God is here.

WAITING FOR WHAT?

The LORD spoke to Moses in the wilderness of Sinai,
in the tent of meeting, on the first day of the second month,
in the second year after they had come out of the land of Egypt.

NUMBERS 1:1, ESV

In 1952, the playwright Samuel Beckett published *Waiting for Godot*, the story of two characters who waited—for the entire length of the play—for a person who would never materialize. Life, Beckett portrayed, was ultimately an empty search. We were all like Estragon and Vladimir, he said, waiting for God to show up, waiting for life to make sense, waiting for who knows what.

As the children of Israel ticked off the days since their exodus from Egypt, they also began to wonder what they were waiting for. The Greek version of the Old Testament, the Septuagint, refers to this part of the biblical story as Numbers, named for its family rosters and lists that act as bookends. However, the Hebrew Scriptures call it something different—*bemidbar*, a word that means "in the wilderness," taken from the first verse of the book. It's not hard to see why. For the next forty years, Israel would wander in the desert. Waiting would be its own wilderness.

Grief includes so much waiting. If we're caregivers, we experience anticipatory grief, a grief that includes waiting as we watch our person die. If our loss involves a crime or unexpected health difficulty, we wait for news that will hopefully bring clarity or resolution. Whatever our loss, we all sit like the Israelites in the desert or Estragon and Vladmir on a park bench, waiting for life to make sense. We wait to feel better, for the hurt to ebb a little. We may be waiting for God to show up too.

Numbers 1 offers a helpful, hopeful reminder: "The LORD spoke to Moses in the wilderness." God did not abandon the Israelites in the desert of their loss. Neither would he make them walk their own paths alone, isolated in wilderness. God showed up for Moses, in Israel's waiting. He'll do the same for you.

Your wilderness isn't meaningless. Your waiting isn't in vain. Quite to the contrary, this landscape of loss that feels so foreboding is infused with divine Presence. God is here. God wants to commune with you. However long it takes for the waiting to end, he will stay beside you. He will faithfully lead you to the fulfillment of his promises.

Because of your great compassion you did not abandon them in the wilderness. By day the pillar of cloud did not fail to guide them on their path, nor the pillar of fire by night to shine on the way they were to take. You gave your good Spirit to instruct them. You did not withhold your manna from their mouths, and you gave them water for their thirst. For forty years you sustained them in the wilderness; they lacked nothing, their clothes did not wear out nor did their feet become swollen.

NEHEMIAH 9:19-21, NIV

Haven't I commanded you? Strength! Courage! Don't be timid; don't get discouraged. GOD, your God, is with you every step you take.

JOSHUA 1:9, MSG

A Prayer: God, I'm left in limbo between the life I lived before and who knows what. I don't know what's ahead, and I keep waiting for this wilderness to be over. Sometimes, I confess I even start to wonder where you are—if you're good, strong, or powerful. Forgive me for my unbelief and strengthen my faith. Help me to endure this wilderness, and speak words of comfort to reassure me of your love. Root me in the truth that this wandering won't last forever. Amen.

An Activity for Today: Block out time to wander today. Choose a safe route—around your office park, through your neighborhood, in a favorite big-box store—and simply wander. Consciously leave your mental agenda behind. Don't wear a watch. Invite God to wander with you. As you walk, consider how open-ended, mindful wandering can open up your creativity, refresh your spiritual life, or give you hope. What do you notice as you walk? Does your body feel different as you move? Do you find ideas flow more freely? Does God feel just a little bit closer? Thomas Merton once prayed, "My God, I pray better to you by breathing, I pray better to you by walking than by talking."[5] Let this be your prayer today too. God is in your wilderness waiting and wandering.

A Song to Encourage Your Heart: "No Vacant Thrones" by Phillip Joubert and Jonni Mae

Our big problems don't faze God a bit. Instead, each problem presents an opportunity for God to display his power and goodness in our lives.

LARGER THAN LIFE

*They said, ". . . All the people we saw there are of
great size. . . . We seemed like grasshoppers in our
own eyes, and we looked the same to them."*

NUMBERS 13:32-33, NIV

On Sunday, May 3, 2020, the *Guardian* reported, "Icelandic
actor and strongman Hafthor Bjornsson set a world record for
the deadlift on Saturday when he lifted 1,104 lb (501 kg), over
half a metric tonne, at Thor's Power Gym in Iceland."[6] Bjornsson
became arguably the strongest man in the world that day, lifting
the weight of a full-grown cow or a concert grand piano!

Strong men might look impressive on television or in the
gym, but the spies Moses commissioned for reconnaissance in
the Promised Land didn't think they were cool at all. Though
the land bore luscious fruit, the men who returned with reports
for Israel could only talk about giants. Everything about the
Promised Land seemed larger than life. Milk and honey flowed.
Jumbo grapes grew. But overshadowing all of this abundance
stood intimidating opposition—fortified cities, powerful enemies, and very, very big men. Though this was the place to which
God had faithfully led them, Israel saw fear, not favor.

The death of a loved one introduces us to a laundry list of
similarly larger-than-life challenges. Along with the big emotions
that come with grief, many deaths precipitate hard changes in

our lives. Death can bring financial struggles and career changes. It can force your hand on moving to a new place or selling your house. The death of your person may provoke health difficulties or new anxieties. All of these struggles remind us that grief is a weight we cannot carry on our own. It's just too big for us to bear. The obstacles before us can make it hard to trust God.

Thankfully, our big problems don't faze God a bit. Instead, each problem presents an opportunity for God to display his power and goodness in our lives. As you live with grief, you face the giants of fear, scarcity, and change. You must encounter and learn to live in a life you never wanted. Nevertheless, God is still fulfilling his promises in your life, even when you see only fear, not favor. Just as he did for Israel, God will conquer the problems that intimidate you. He will lead you into a land where you can flourish. His good plans for you continue even in this hard season.

The LORD will fulfill his purpose for me; your steadfast love, O LORD, endures forever. Do not forsake the work of your hands.
PSALM 138:8, ESV

My times are in your hands; deliver me from the hands of my enemies, from those who pursue me. Let your face shine on your servant; save me in your unfailing love.
PSALM 31:15-16, NIV

A Prayer: God, everything since my person died feels too heavy for me to handle. I can't carry the weight of my grief, and giant problems have arisen in my life because of loss. I feel so weak. Remind me today that you are with me, that none of this surprises you. Recall to my heart your faithfulness in my past, and open my eyes to see your provision in my present. Reassure me of the good future you have laid out for me. Come today and defeat my giants for me. Let me "sing in the shadow of your wings" (Psalm 63:7). Amen.

An Activity for Today: Carrying the memory of your person can feel like a weighty task. There's so much to remember, so many little moments and details. How will you ever capture all of who your person was to you? Below, create an acrostic with your person's name that articulates some of the qualities you loved best about your person. As you identify each word, remember a particular moment when that quality was on display and meditate on its influence in your life. (For example, perhaps your Uncle Bob's **b**oldness, **o**bstinance, and **b**ravery taught you to keep at it when the going was rough.) Save your acrostic and use it to introduce your loved one to someone who may not have known them well.

A Song to Encourage Your Heart: "Yet Not I but through Christ in Me" by CityAlight

Until Jesus returns, your loss

will hurt. As you wait for

that day, God offers you the

unexpected healing power

of his presence in your pain.

STRANGE HEALING

*The LORD said to Moses, "Make a snake and put it up
on a pole; anyone who is bitten can look at it and live."*

NUMBERS 21:8, NIV

One summer afternoon, my boys were playing in the backyard of
a friend's house. Suddenly, my son burst into the house holding
his hand. "A bee stung me," he announced as he clutched his red
palm. Lickety-split, my friend hopped up and opened a kitchen
drawer. She shuffled through items until she found what she was
looking for—a tiny bottle of pure lavender oil.

I'd seen lavender used in sachets, neck pillows, and lotions, but
I'd never seen its amazing healing powers until that day. This little
flower that attracts bees and blooms so beautifully in backyards can
also soothe an insect sting. What incredible, unexpected healing!

In Numbers 21, the children of Israel grumbled against Moses
as they traveled in the desert, and the Lord brought venomous
snakes to bite them as punishment for their sin. When the people
realized their wrongdoing, the Lord saw their repentance and
answered with an unexpected kind of healing. A bronze snake on
a pole would remind the people of God's healing forgiveness. All
they had to do was raise their eyes to be cured.

What a strange healing God offered! He didn't take away the
snakes, but he offered something better than merely physical healing. God offered what the Israelites really needed—an opportunity
for restored relationship with him. Healing lay exclusively in their

connection with the Great Physician, the one who could remedy the sin-sickness that was their real and greater injury.

When people talk about grief, they often use the word *healing* for the resolution of the pain we feel. But grief isn't something that heals like a broken arm or a bee sting. You can't set a bone, apply ointment, or try to keep the wound clean of grief. To live fully after loss, we must accept this reality. However, that doesn't mean you can't experience the redemptive healing care of God in your life with loss today.

Until Jesus returns, your loss will hurt. As you wait for that day, God offers you the unexpected healing power of his presence in your pain. All you have to do is raise your eyes. What will God's healing power look like in your life? Like lavender oil on a bee sting, you can expect it might be subtle. It will require constant application of his life-giving resurrection truth to your heart. God's healing power won't take away all of the pain today, but the sweet-smelling aroma of his presence will remind you that sorrow can live side by side with joy. As you wait for Christ to come again, God offers you healing of a different kind. Not the "get over it and move on" kind that the world sells, but a quiet trust that gently soothes your heartbreak and offers you fresh new mercies for this day.

Heal me, LORD, and I will be healed; save me and I will be saved, for you are the one I praise.
JEREMIAH 17:14, NIV

Gracious words are a honeycomb, sweet to the soul and healing to the bones.
PROVERBS 16:24, NIV

A Prayer: *Lord Jesus, you were lifted up like the bronze serpent to save me from death's pain. Today, I look to you for the kind of healing only you can give. I do not expect my grief to go away this side of heaven, but I do pray that you would be present with me in it. Soothe my sadness with your love. Encourage my heart with your provision. Heal my hope as you bring me new life each day. I trust that someday you will return to make all things new. I long for that day when complete healing arrives for me and for those I love. Come quickly, Lord Jesus. I wait for you. Amen.*

An Activity for Today: *While ultimate healing will only come when Jesus returns, we can experience a foretaste of that goodness in the company of others. If you haven't done so already, sign up for a grief support group and enter a community of care. Hospice organizations often offer relationship-specific loss groups (young widows, parents with children, siblings, etc.). Many churches offer grief support that doesn't require you to be a member of the congregation. Visit www.GriefShare.org to find a community group that makes you feel less alone and supports you as you learn to live without your person.*

A Song to Encourage Your Heart: *"Praise before My Breakthrough" by Bryan and Katie Torwalt*

In our suffering and tragedy,

God has important things

to say, if we will only stop

and listen.

ARE YOU LISTENING?

When the donkey saw the angel of the LORD, it lay down under
Balaam, and he was angry and beat it with his staff. Then
the LORD opened the donkey's mouth, and it said to Balaam,
"What have I done to you to make you beat me these three times?"

NUMBERS 22:27-28, NIV

God created animals to communicate with each other in amazing ways. Whales intonate information to each other regarding
their whereabouts. Birds flutter their wings in elaborate mating
rituals to say, "I'm available! Let's go on a date!" However, none
of us would ever expect our beloved dog or cat to open its mouth
and talk.

The prophet Balaam didn't expect that either. But on the
road to Moab, he got the surprise of his life. Balaam had been
tasked with a difficult assignment, to oppose Israel's God and
curse the nation on behalf of its enemies. However, God had
other plans in mind. Who better to help deliver God's message
than Balaam's donkey!

As she loped along the road toward Moab, Balaam's donkey
behaved strangely three times. When she saw an angel of the
Lord standing in the road, invisible to Balaam, she ran off into
a field until Balaam beat her back to the road. Next, to get by
the angel, the donkey slid against a stone wall, crushing Balaam's
foot. Finally, when other attempts had failed to dissuade Balaam

from his intentions, the donkey opened her mouth and spoke! At last, Balaam would pay attention. What an odd and unexpected wake-up call!

The death of a loved one wakes us up from our illusions too. We travel along through life with our own intentions, when loss stops us in our tracks. Like Balaam, we stand in the middle of the road, confused and angry. What in the world is happening? Death is like Balaam's donkey, calling out for us to pay attention. In our suffering and tragedy, God has important things to say, if we will only stop and listen.

Rather than plug your ears and cover your eyes, invite your loss to reveal God's truth to you. Do you need a wake-up call to reorder your priorities? Have relationships fallen by the wayside that need strengthening now? What do you see differently now since your loss? God can speak in unexpected ways. Ask him to open your eyes, ears, and heart to his word for you today.

I will listen to what God the LORD says; he promises peace to his people, his faithful servants—but let them not turn to folly.
PSALM 85:8, NIV

It is the LORD your God you must follow, and him you must revere. Keep his commands and obey him; serve him and hold fast to him.
DEUTERONOMY 13:4, NIV

A Prayer: God, I confess that I often floated along in life before my loss, but death has shaken me awake. I don't want to miss this opportunity to listen, learn, and grow. Open my eyes to see your work around me. Train my ears to hear your voice. Teach my heart to respond when you instruct and guide me. I am yours, God. Shape me more today into your likeness. Amen.

An Activity for Today: Make a playlist that reminds you of your person. Include songs that your person liked and that you enjoyed together and those that make you think about him or her. Think about how the genre and lyrics can speak for the emotions you hold inside. Listen to your playlist when you need to feel close to your person. Music can offer needed catharsis, so it's okay if the songs bring tears. If you feel comfortable, share your playlist with a friend as a way of communicating what's in your head and heart. Sometimes music says how we feel better than our own words ever could.

A Song to Encourage Your Heart: "I Am Thine, O Lord" by Grace Brumley

In joy and in grief, God asks

for our whole hearts.

No matter what happens,

he calls us to love him

first and best of all.

ALL OF ME LOVES ALL OF YOU

Hear, O Israel: The LORD our God, the LORD is one.
Love the LORD your God with all your heart and
with all your soul and with all your strength.

DEUTERONOMY 6:4-5, NIV

Did you know "Sanskrit has ninety-six words for love; ancient Persian has eighty, Greek three, and English only one"?[7] If English is your first language and you've struggled with words to express your loss, is it any wonder? With few words to express this deepest emotion, it's hard to sum up all the ways you treasure and miss your person. Vocabulary is so limited! How do simple human words ever adequately convey what it means to have your person die?

The death of a loved one reveals to us the fullness of our emotions for that person. Those who experience the death of a challenging family member long for restored love. Those who enjoyed a friend's intimacy in life now long for it in death's separation. Death does not destroy love, but it does reshape how we're able to express it. We may understand for the first time how our love for our person has infused everything we do, think, and say in life.

When Moses met with God to receive the Ten Commandments, God handed him two stones carved in love. These words expressed God's love for his people. The Ten Commandments instructed Israel about how to live holy lives, but God wasn't just interested in particulars—a world with no murder, stealing, or Sabbath-breaking. God never wanted his people to mix up the language of law with the language of love.

Above loving their spouses, their parents, their servants, or their neighbors, God wanted them to love him best of all. Rote compliance with a list of commandments could never prompt that kind of affection. So God made it clear. He commanded Israel to love him with everything: their hearts, their souls, and their minds. When they allowed God's presence into every corner of their lives, Israel would communicate clearly their love for him.

As grieving Christians, God calls us to hold fast to our love for him even as we continue to love those who have died. In our mourning, all of our earthly loves should direct our affections toward God. In joy and in grief, God asks for our whole hearts. No matter what happens, he calls us to love him first and best of all.

What would it look like for you to move beyond compliance in your relationship with God? How could you express the inexpressible—the lavish kindness that God has poured out abundantly on you through Jesus? Your person's influence and memory infuses your life and brings meaning to it. How much more can God's presence produce good things as you invite him into your heart, soul, and mind? Today, ask God to help you love him with every part of you.

———

Guard your heart above all else, for it determines the course of your life.
PROVERBS 4:23, NLT

How priceless is your unfailing love, O God! People take refuge in the shadow of your wings.
PSALM 36:7, NIV

A Prayer: Dear Jesus, my loss has revealed to me how much love I had to give. Without my person, I'm not sure where all that love should go or how it can be expressed. I realize that this love I carry is only a shadow of the love you've called me to offer you in thanksgiving. Today, Lord Jesus, help me to love you best. Let my loss break open my heart so that I give it more freely to you. Possess every part of me—heart, mind, soul, and strength. I desire to love you with everything I have. Amen.

An Activity for Today: Loving and losing someone is an exhausting experience, and the weariness doesn't just go away. Today, as an act of self-love, lie down for fifteen minutes and take a nap. Find a dark, quiet place to rest. Set a timer on your phone, and simply close your eyes. If you fall asleep, great! If you don't, the rest can still count as restorative. We commend ourselves to God as we slip into the vulnerability of rest, and we rejoice in God's sustaining grace as we rise. Let these normal rhythms remind you that God holds all of your days in his hands. You are always in his care, whether waking or sleeping.

A Song to Encourage Your Heart: "You Love Me Best" by Ellie Holcomb

The words we speak about

our loved ones matter,

not just for us but for those

who come after us.

LAST WORDS

*There has never been another prophet in Israel like
Moses, whom the LORD knew face to face.*

DEUTERONOMY 34:10, NLT

When the famous actor Mel Blanc died, he left behind a host
of characters who had come alive through his voice. We know
Bugs Bunny, Yosemite Sam, and Daffy Duck because of this
"man of 1000 voices," the epitaph written on his gravestone. It is
said that Mel requested a single line added to his stone upon his
death—"That's all folks." As he considered the words that would
outlive him, those two phrases seemed to sum it up.

Whether you've been tasked with writing an obituary or
eulogy or you've had the difficult job of meeting with the funeral
home to determine a gravestone, you've had to consider what
words will sum up your person's life. The task brings lots of pressure to get it right. After all, we've got only one opportunity to
give a eulogy, and once the carving is made, it's tough to change
a cemetery stone. What are the most important things to say
about a person when he or she dies?

The last few chapters of Deuteronomy, which chronicle Moses'
death, were clearly written by someone else God had inspired for
the task. These chapters document Moses' last words of blessing
and instruction to the Israelites. They tell us the story of Moses'
death and the grieving that came afterward. These chapters are

the reflective recollections of a person who missed their leader and wanted to get the words right to remember him. In doing so, they offer us excellent instruction for our own expressions of grief.

First, the writer is honest about Moses' physical condition. Deuteronomy 34:7 tells us that Moses retained his vigor until the end, a comment that reminds us that God sometimes receives our loved ones in the prime of their lives. Second, we learn about Moses' spiritual life. He and his Lord were on intimate terms. The rest of the chapter offers no laundry list of human accomplishments. Instead, the "mighty power" and "awesome deeds" Moses performed are celebrated as work done through the God who had sent him (Deuteronomy 34:12, NIV).

Have you been tasked with crafting words about your loved one? Would it be helpful to write your own words privately as part of your grieving process? These last chapters of Deuteronomy remind us that the words we speak about our loved ones matter, not just for us but for those who come after us. The ritual of remembering can help you crystallize your thoughts and verbalize your grief in ways that you might not do otherwise. As you give shape to words, whether aloud or on paper, you recall God's faithfulness and grieve with hope.

———

I will remember the deeds of the LORD; yes, I will remember your wonders of old.

PSALM 77:11, ESV

Let all that I am praise the LORD; may I never forget the good things he does for me.

PSALM 103:2, NLT

A Prayer: *God, sometimes I don't even want to sit long enough to remember my person specifically. I'm afraid that all the memories will rush in and overwhelm me. I realize, however, that I need the time to remember my loss. I need to rehearse the details of their life so that I can say goodbye. Help me in this task so that I don't become lost in my emotions. Give me grace to face the hard memories. Give me joy as I recall the good times. Help me find the words to say the things that need to be said—honestly, lovingly, and in a way that always glorifies you. Amen.*

An Activity for Today: *In the space below, write your own short eulogy for your person. It's okay to sit with both the happy and hard parts of your person's story. What is the lasting testimony of your person's life, beyond his or her worldly accomplishments? What will you remember most about him or her? You don't need to be a great writer. This is a reflective exercise to help you grieve. Whether or not you were able to deliver a formal eulogy at the funeral service, this eulogy can give you an opportunity to say the things that you need to say.*

_____

_____

_____

_____

_____

_____

_____

A Song to Encourage Your Heart: *"Remembers Me (Psalm 105)" by Mike Janzen*

God's faithfulness doesn't just chase after us; it goes before us too. Behind and before and beside, God walks with us into our new lives after loss.

STARTING OVER

*Joshua told the people, "Consecrate yourselves, for tomorrow
the LORD will do amazing things among you."*

JOSHUA 3:5, NIV

When I was in my early twenties, my mother taught me to
knit. We sat together, needles in hand, and she taught me the
steady pattern of looping over and pulling through. As I found
my rhythm, I began to pick up speed. I enjoyed the repetitive
motion—that is, until I lost count of my stitches! I added here
and dropped there, and before I knew it, my simple scarf had
bulges and holes galore.

"You'll need to rip out your stitches back to where you can
restart," my mom told me when she saw my work. Her instruction
busted a hole in my enthusiasm. Rip out my work and start over?
Wasn't there an easier way? I'd made rows of stitches. Now I'd need
to do them all over, erasing everything I'd accomplished thus far?

Unfortunately, like my first scarf, beginning again after the
death of your person means a complete overhaul. Daily routines
must change, thought patterns must change. You need to replace
the emergency contact on your health forms. You must stop
grabbing your phone to text your loved one when you have a
thought you want to share. You must learn new skills, file painful
paperwork. Nothing about starting over is easy.

After Moses' death, God tasked the Israelites' new leader,
Joshua, with leading the people into the Promised Land. It was a

hopeful new beginning but also a painful starting over. Sin had kept the Israelites trapped in the wilderness, and in this new land they'd need to rip out the old habits and reconstruct new lives wholly committed to God.

As they stood on the shore of the Jordan River, Joshua shouted, "Get ready! Tomorrow God's going to do amazing things for you!" The people knew God's character and track record. Still, as they stood at the edge of their new lives, they needed reassurance that God's power and provision in their lives didn't stop at the sandy edge of the desert. It went ahead of them, into tomorrow, preparing a way for their flourishing.

The same goes for you and me as we face our own starting overs. God's faithfulness doesn't just chase after us; it goes before us too. Behind and before and beside, God walks with us into our new lives after loss. As you begin the painful, unwelcome rhythms of unraveling and starting over, you can trust that God is there with you. He will guide, comfort, and strengthen you to do the work he has placed before you.

———

The LORD himself goes before you and will be with you; he will never leave you nor forsake you. Do not be afraid; do not be discouraged.
DEUTERONOMY 31:8, NIV

If I climb to the sky, you're there! If I go underground, you're there! If I flew on morning's wings to the far western horizon, you'd find me in a minute—you're already there waiting! Then I said to myself, "Oh, he even sees me in the dark! At night I'm immersed in the light!" It's a fact: darkness isn't dark to you; night and day, darkness and light, they're all the same to you.
PSALM 139:8-12, MSG

A Prayer: *Dear Jesus, I don't want to begin again. I liked my life before my loss, and starting over feels so painful without my person here beside me. I know that you are with me wherever I go, so today I ask that you walk with me through my starting over. Remind me of your presence when I have to do something new. Assure me of your strength when I need to learn a skill or grow in an area I find difficult. Show me your amazing work in my life to encourage my heart. Amen.*

An Activity for Today: *Athletes coming back from injury all start in the same place: they stretch. Gentle exercise like this primes stiff joints and loosens tight muscles. Stretching lengthens and strengthens, preparing the body for more rigorous engagement to come. Today, as an act of starting over, spend some time in gentle stretching. Watch a stretching video on YouTube, or simply do what you know—raising your arms above your head, touching your toes, and spreading your arms out like birds' wings. As you stretch, recall that God has committed to renewing your strength like the eagle's as you hope in him (see Isaiah 40:31). Breathe, feel your body move, and pray aloud, "My hope is in you."*

A Song to Encourage Your Heart: *"Let Me Find Thee" by Matthew Smith*

God's testimony of faithfulness

will last forever. Like the

memorials Joshua built

in the Promised Land,

the altars to God's glory

that we build in our grief

will never crumble away.

I'LL BE AROUND

*Joshua set up the twelve stones that had been in the middle of
the Jordan at the spot where the priests who carried the ark
of the covenant had stood. And they are there to this day.*

JOSHUA 4:9, NIV

All across small New England towns, monuments stand on quiet
town greens memorializing lost soldiers. Long ago stonecutters
carved into small granite obelisks the names of local boys who
fought and never came home—from the American Revolution,
the War Between the States, World Wars I and II. On an average
summer afternoon, these monuments stand in silent testimony as
kids throw footballs and families picnic. Many names are known
now only to genealogy buffs, but nobody would ever think of
taking the monuments down. After all these years, those names
still matter.

Throughout the Old Testament, the people of God created
altars and monuments at places where God met and sustained
them. It's not much of a surprise, then, that here, as the Israelites
crossed the Jordan into their new home in Canaan, Joshua built
a monument to commemorate the moment. The event called for
celebration and remembrance. For as long as people came down
to the Jordan to water their cattle or wash their clothes, they'd see
the stone pile and recall God's care.

While the creation of this monument made sense at the

moment, the author of Joshua included an interesting phrase that he repeats elsewhere in the book: "And they are there to this day." Years after God's miraculous acts, the monuments still stood. Generations later, when the particular names and faces had been forgotten, the testimony of God's presence and provision still summoned the people to awe and praise. These altars weren't to recall the Israelites' victories but God's.

Much of grief work is monument building. We remember our loved one and create monuments—physical and emotional—to cement our people forever in our hearts and memories. We're worried we'll forget, so we save their clothes and create photo albums and form nonprofits. But like all human endeavors, these mini memorials will fade and crumble with time. Their importance will be forgotten, like those obelisks in New England towns that few will even stop to look at.

Our passage today offers us a hopeful contrast, however. God's testimony of faithfulness will last forever. Like the memorials Joshua built in the Promised Land, the altars to God's glory that we build in our grief will never crumble away. As you grieve the loss of your person, consider the altars and memorials you are building today. Whose work are you celebrating? Let your grief manifest worship for our unchanging, almighty God.

I remember the days of long ago; I meditate on all your works and consider what your hands have done.
PSALM 143:5, NIV

I have set the LORD always before me; because he is at my right hand, I shall not be shaken.
PSALM 16:8, ESV

A Prayer: *God, I miss my person. I want to keep and create and build things that last to remind me always of him/her. I'm afraid that I will forget and that my person will be forgotten. Keep me from unhealthy striving to preserve what has been lost. Remind me that all people are like grass that withers, but you, Lord, last forever. Open my eyes to your work all around me, and give me the courage to build memorials to you above all others. Don't let me forget how good you have been and always will be to me. Amen.*

An Activity for Today: *Get creative and draw! In the blank space on this page, create two monuments—one to your person and one to God's work in your life. Monuments signify our accomplishments, but they also mark moments in time. Think creatively here, and don't let your drawing skills (or lack thereof!) inhibit you. What shape will your monuments be? What writing will be on them? In what context will you place them? Let this artistic exercise open your heart to a deeper understanding of God's goodness. Let it be a celebration, not only of your person, but also of the God who promises to never leave you.*

A Song to Encourage Your Heart: *"Come Thou Fount of Every Blessing" by Eclipse 6*

Though the darkness

now feels deep,

someday you'll look out

over your life

and see how far

you've come.

THE TEMPTATION
OF LIVING WITH LOSS

*I handed you a land for which you did not work, towns you
did not build. And here you are now living in them and
eating from vineyards and olive groves you did not plant.*

JOSHUA 24:13, MSG

Since Senator Henry Clay spoke the words in 1842, the American
imagination has been captivated by the idea of the "self-made
man." We all love a rags-to-riches story. We're conditioned from
childhood to rub a little dirt in our wounds and get back in the
game. We celebrate grit and the achievements that come with it.

Certainly, perseverance and tenacity are character qualities to be
honored. Our world needs people who keep their word and stick
with tough tasks until the very end. But if you think this method
will serve you well in grief, you've got a rude awakening coming.

As Joshua neared the end of his life and ministry years, he
called the Israelites together to offer his parting words. Much like
his predecessor Moses, Joshua wanted to leave the people with
important instructions about what to do next. They'd only just
begun their new lives in the Promised Land. There was so much
left to do to make this place the space God dreamed for it to be.
Conquer enemies, build cities, cultivate the land so it flourishes.

As Joshua instructed the people, he didn't just give them a to-
do list of practical tasks. He reminded them of the temptations
that come with building. It's easy to get distracted, he warned.

It's easy to wrongly prioritize. Most of all, when you begin to see your new life rise beautifully before you, it will be easy to think you've done it all yourself. Eventually, Joshua knew that day would come. So he reminded the people: when you look at the richness of your life, remember that God has done it all.

One of the greatest temptations of living with loss is the subtle belief that sneaks in around our grief. We develop new friendships, rebuild our careers, and reconnect with activities that used to give us joy. As our lives grow around our loss, we can fall into the trap of the self-made man, believing we've done this all ourselves. People tell us, "You're so strong," and while we know it's not true, we begin to forget that anything we've accomplished is only by God's amazing grace.

Though the darkness now feels deep, someday you'll look out over your life and see how far you've come. You'll be tempted to think like the Israelites that this land you've cultivated is yours alone, that the olive groves and fields of your flourishing are due to your own stick-to-itiveness. Before that day comes, commit now to glorifying God for his work in your life. Every single moment of your survival and thriving after loss is a gift from him. Whether you realize it or not, that starts today.

―――――

Not to us, O LORD, not to us, but to your name give glory, for the sake of your steadfast love and your faithfulness!
PSALM 115:1, ESV

Since ancient times no one has heard, no ear has perceived, no eye has seen any God besides you, who acts on behalf of those who wait for him.
ISAIAH 64:4, NIV

A Prayer: God, all things come from you; nothing I hold in my hands is my own. Remind me of this truth as I rebuild my life today. Keep me from the temptation of the self-made man. I want to create a life after loss that honors my love for my person and honors you most of all. In everything I do today, let my life give you praise. Amen.

An Activity for Today: Rain or shine, it's time for a sound walk today. Psalm 19 tells us that the heavens declare God's glory. Creation has a voice, and your task is to listen to it sing today.

On your walk, first focus on the man-made sounds—cars moving past, lawn mowers humming, helicopters hovering. Thank God for his creativity manifested in the people he has made. All of those noises we consider loud (and sometimes obnoxious) are made by living, breathing, beloved creatures of God.

Next, listen beyond the human noise for creation's sounds—the wind in the trees, cicadas on neighborhood lawns, birds calling to one another. All of these sing God's praises in the language he gave them. The whole world shouts aloud that God is king, that he is Lord over all. Let this symphony bring you comfort today.

A Song to Encourage Your Heart: "Not to Us" by Chris Tomlin

God has not abandoned

her as she supposed.

Instead, the woman who

grieves is also the woman

who can know joy.

WHAT'S YOUR NAME?

"Don't call me Naomi," she told them.
"Call me Mara, because the Almighty
has made my life very bitter."

Did you grow up with a name nobody could spell or pronounce? Did you ever wish as a child that you could have a different name? I know I did. Even as an adult, I've sometimes struggled with my name. I worked for three years with a woman who regularly called me "Melissa." Eventually, I got tired of correcting her and just let it be.

Even if you've dreamed of calling yourself something else, the reality of a name change is huge. Not only must you file reams of paperwork, but you must also somehow get everyone else around you to start calling you by your new name! If you've changed your name because of marriage or divorce, you know how complicated this seemingly small switch can be.

After Naomi lost her husband and two sons in quick succession, she wanted a name change. Her given name meant "sweetness," but life had turned sour in a way she'd never expected. Nothing about her name seemed to fit her situation, and her name certainly didn't reflect the person she felt she was now. When her friends welcomed her back to her hometown after years away, Naomi asked them to call her Mara instead, a name that meant "bitter." Considering the disaster that had befallen her, Naomi thought the name was a better fit.

Each of us experiences an identity change after loss. You may be the oldest sibling now after being the middle child. You may be a widow or widower. You may be an orphan, having lost both of your parents. You may be a friend who feels like her sidekick is gone. However death shifts your relationships with others, it also changes your relationship with yourself. Loss renames you, and it hurts. You knew who you were before. Now you must find a new name.

Naomi's preferred name, "Mara," fit for a little while. For most of the book of Ruth, we watch Naomi grieve and plod along, facing each day with little enthusiasm for the tasks that lie ahead. Bitterness is her cup as she mourns her loss. However, as we read her story, we learn that Mara and Naomi are two names for the same woman. God has not abandoned her as she supposed. Instead, the woman who grieves is also the woman who can know joy. The last time we meet Naomi, she's holding her baby grandson in her arms—a wild dream come true after so much heartache. She is learning to carry the bitterness and the sweetness in the same hand.

What would you call yourself today? Is your name Bitter? Despair? Longing? Tell God your name today, and ask him to give you a new name beyond the darkness of your grief. Whatever names you give yourself, to God, you are always called "Beloved." His faithful love will hold you as your name and your identity change.

Now, this is what the LORD says—he who created you, Jacob, he who formed you, Israel: "Do not fear, for I have redeemed you; I have summoned you by name; you are mine."

ISAIAH 43:1, NIV

You have turned for me my mourning into dancing; you have loosed my sackcloth and clothed me with gladness.

PSALM 30:11, ESV

A Prayer: *Jesus, my loss has changed so much in my life that I struggle to recognize myself in the mirror. Sometimes I don't know who I am anymore. Even my name doesn't fit me like it used to. I believe that you have named me as your child and that your banner over me is love. As I go through this day, remind me of my truest name—Beloved of God—and help me to receive this name as my life's supply. Let what you call me define me more than the names I give myself. Amen.*

An Activity for Today: *Imagine that your grief has a name. What is it today? Did it have a different name yesterday? Take a few moments with your eyes closed to picture grief as a person with a name. How does your grief stand and move? What does your grief's face look like? In this quiet moment, introduce your grief to God. Invite them to meet and walk together with you. If your body feels tense, take a deep breath and relax through the exhale. God can befriend your grief when you cannot. He knows its name, and he knows yours too.*

A Song to Encourage Your Heart: *"You Know My Name" by Tasha Cobbs Leonard*

Naomi knew from her own life's experience that slowly placing one foot in front of the other was the only way to move with sorrow.

FACING YOUR STACK OF PANCAKES

*Wash, put on perfume, and get dressed in your best
clothes. Then go down to the threshing floor.*

RUTH 3:3, NIV

Years ago, my husband and I took our daughter to a restaurant
for breakfast. We knew she was hungry, but when the waitress
placed a steaming plate of pancakes before our little girl, she
didn't pick up her fork. She didn't even seem hungry anymore.
What had happened?

After encouraging her to eat for a few minutes, my husband
had an idea. He lifted two of the pancakes off the plate, leaving only one behind. Cutting the single pancake into pieces, he
encouraged her again. "Go ahead and eat." She picked up her
fork and gobbled down her meal, only to ask for more. She'd
simply had too much on her plate to know what to do next.

I'm sure you've felt like that at times since your person died.
All of the details and the emotions stack up like pancakes on a
plate, and you're not sure where to start. Do you cut into the
paperwork or lie down and take a nap? Do you focus on getting
the closets cleaned out, or do you thumb through photo albums
and drink in the memories? It can be incredibly hard to know
what to do when your head is in the disorienting fog of grief.

Naomi and her daughter-in-law Ruth existed in that same fog. Naomi's three losses compounded her grief, while Ruth experienced both grief and change as she left her own people to move to a new city. Nevertheless, Naomi did something wise in Ruth chapter three that invites us to healthy grieving and growth after loss. She instructed Ruth to do her next right thing.

Notice Naomi's instructions to her daughter-in-law: take care of your body, move, complete a task. Three simple commands, each one a challenge in the face of her sorrow. And yet Naomi knew from her own life's experience that slowly placing one foot in front of the other was the only way to move with sorrow.

Hudson Taylor, the missionary to China who saw his own fair share of sorrow, once said, "If we are faithful to God in little things, we shall gain experience and strength that will be helpful to us in the more serious trials of life." Today, do a small job that stands before you. Eat one pancake at a time. As you do, ask God to join you in the simple tasks of your day. He will impart encouragement in even the smallest details so that you are strengthened to face your life after loss.

———

LORD, you establish peace for us; all that we have accomplished you have done for us.

ISAIAH 26:12, NIV

May the favor of the Lord our God rest on us; establish the work of our hands for us—yes, establish the work of our hands.

PSALM 90:17, NIV

A Prayer: God, so many responsibilities and emotions have piled up because of my loss. I'm not sure where to start. I feel overwhelmed with all the work to do, the relationships to mend and strengthen, my emotions and body to care for. Show me today what the one needful thing is. Enlighten my eyes to see what you have placed before me to do. Give me wisdom to discern where I need to work and where I need to rest, and strengthen me for the task. Remind me to place all of my efforts into your hands. You will do more than I can ask or think according to your great riches in Christ Jesus. Amen.

An Activity for Today: Have you offered yourself condolences since your person died? No, really. Have you told yourself, "I'm sorry for your loss"? Today, take a moment to extend your sympathies to yourself—yes, you. If you have trouble putting words together, hop over to a discount store and buy yourself a card. (Or remake one that has been sent to you!) What are the words you would say to yourself about the experience of losing your loved one? What compassion, love, and tenderness can you give to yourself? Hint: you may be surprised to discover that the platitudes others have offered fall flat when you extend them to yourself. As you consider these unhelpful words, think about the loving sentiments that stand behind them. Say those things to yourself instead. You've been through a lot; you deserve kindness from yourself too.

A Song to Encourage Your Heart: "Your Labor Is Not in Vain" by The Porter's Gate

God never gives up on

communicating with his

beloved children—through

his Word, through prayer,

and through his church.

CLEANING OUT OUR EARS

*Eli realized that the L*ORD *was calling the boy. So Eli
told Samuel, "Go and lie down, and if he calls you,
say, 'Speak, L*ORD, *for your servant is listening.'"*

1 SAMUEL 3:8-9, NIV

Did you know that earwax plays an important role in our bodies'
health? Like a guardian at an entrance, earwax traps dust and dirt
before they can travel further into the ear canal and do real damage. Its oily consistency is a first line of defense against bacteria
that cause infection.

Sometimes, however, this amazing little creation of God
works overtime in production. Earwax builds up, and the blockage gives you a headache or, worse, begins to obscure your hearing. If sounds are muffled and you sometimes feel dizzy, you
might need to clean out your ears.

The priest Eli was one man who had a similar ear problem.
Eli served in God's Temple faithfully for many years. Israel's sin
created a barrier to approaching God's holiness, so God had
appointed Eli to act in their place. Every day, Eli worked in service
of the Lord, cleaning the Temple, offering sacrifices, and helping
people figure out how to approach the God he knew so well.

However, when we encounter Eli in 1 Samuel 3, it appears
his ears are a little clogged. Israel's repeated sin had led to an
uncomfortable silence in their relationship with God. Their

senses were clogged by temptations and sinful living, so much so that when God came to speak to the young Samuel in the Temple one night, even Eli couldn't recognize his voice.

When Samuel heard God speaking in the night, he ran to Eli, and twice Eli sent him back to bed. Only the third time did Eli realize what Samuel was experiencing—a special visit from God. As sin built up in Israel's "ear canals," even Eli's hearing had suffered. He needed God's persistent communication to break through and clear the blockage to his heart.

The same ailment that befell Eli can afflict us in grief. Sin and sorrow can fill our ears with anger, temptation, and self-pity. As we focus solely on earthly things, we may lose our attentiveness to the voice of God in our lives. We may lament God's seeming silence, when really it's *our* ears that need the cleaning.

In our own distraction and frailty, the story of Eli reminds us that, even when we don't recognize his voice, God is still speaking. He never gives up on communicating with his beloved children—through his Word, through prayer, and through his church. As you follow God in your grief, be sure to keep your ears—and your heart—open so that his words of comfort, direction, and love can travel deep into your soul.

Listen to advice and accept instruction, that you may gain wisdom in the future.
PROVERBS 19:20, ESV

The eyes of the LORD are on the righteous, and his ears are attentive to their cry.
PSALM 34:15, NIV

A Prayer: God, I confess that I may need to have my ears cleaned. The temptations that come with grief and the sin that I harbor in my heart—these can block my ears from hearing your goodness spoken over me. Today, teach me to listen to your voice. Open my ears to hear your truth in Scripture, in prayer, and in the witness of your faithful people around me. Help me to not only listen but do what you tell me to do. Amen.

An Activity for Today: Some churches use candle lighting as a visual reminder of the prayers that are offered by a congregation. Today, light a candle in memory of your person. Keep your candle lit throughout the day. Burn it at dinnertime. Use it as part of your personal devotional time. As you light your candle, first remember that Christ our Light will never leave or forsake us. He lights our darkness and guides our feet. Next, take time to recall the light your person brought to your life. Remember his or her laughter, smile, or wisdom. Let the quiet flame bring those memories to mind. Before snuffing out the candle, its own symbolic gesture, thank God for the life of your loved one.

A Song to Encourage Your Heart: "Trust in You" by Lauren Daigle

Your problems are big,

bigger than you ever

expected. But God is big too.

Bigger, perhaps, than you've

ever believed he could be.

BIG PROBLEMS, BIGGER GOD

*The LORD who rescued me from the paw of the lion and the paw
of the bear will rescue me from the hand of this Philistine.*

1 SAMUEL 17:37, NIV

Things always take longer than you expect. It's a reminder that
should be printed in big, bold letters on every instruction manual for home repairs.

Small home repairs often take longer than we expect because
improvement projects can uncover larger, previously hidden
problems. A renovation of the bathroom uncovers mold that
requires remediation, or a deck project reveals cracks in your
home's foundation. Small problems can become big ones in a
split second.

When David arrived at Israel's camp to bring his brothers
food for dinner, he didn't anticipate becoming a warrior for his
people. He was just a boy performing his delivery responsibility.
Hungry bellies may have been the presenting problem, but as
David wandered through the camp, he realized the problems were
actually much bigger. The Philistines' mighty soldier Goliath was
mocking their nation and their God.

If you run up against a home improvement snafu, you've
got two choices: fix it or forget about it. As he stood listening to
Goliath's taunts, David realized he had the same decision to make.
But like a homeowner standing before a flooded bathroom, David

understood the problem that faced him was bigger than anything he could handle alone. Yes, the problem needed fixing. Yet this was the biggest challenge David had ever faced. How could he face a giant?

You've got your own giants in life after loss, problems that seem too big to fix alone. You've got financial struggles, friendship tensions, and physical challenges. Your future feels uncertain, and your past is inaccessible. You're stressed that it's taking longer than you expected to feel secure or happy or healthy again. Like David, grief has uncovered big problems that you don't know how to face.

Today, let David's testimony guide you as you face your own giants. As he stood on the cusp of heading into battle against Goliath, David recited God's mighty acts on his behalf. Just as God had fought for him in the past, God would fight for him now.

In the same way, God will fight for you today. Your problems are big, bigger than you ever expected. But God is big too. Bigger, perhaps, than you've ever believed he could be. Today, place your problems in his hands. They may take longer to resolve than you hope, but you can trust God's workmanship. He's the Master Renovator.

Clearly, you are a God who works behind the scenes, God of Israel, Savior God.
ISAIAH 45:15, MSG

The LORD himself will fight for you. Just stay calm.
EXODUS 14:14, NLT

A Prayer: *God, the death of my person has brought problems into my life that I never expected. Some of them I feel like I can handle. Others look like giants in my path. I know that you are faithful and wise and capable. Meet me today in my struggles and show me your strength. Remind me that, however long things take, you are in the work of fixing. You are the restorer of all things. Amen.*

An Activity for Today: *Does grief make you fidgety? Is it hard to concentrate or sit still? Does your mind wander because life feels big and hard right now? Take a cue from the kids around you, and grab yourself a fidget toy. Fidget spinners, pop fidget toys, and mini containers of Play-Doh are all available in discount stores, ready to help alleviate your restlessness. Grab a stress ball to flex during a call with the funeral home or a Rubik's Cube to twist when you're feeling lonely. Some faith traditions use prayer beads to focus the mind and heart on God. A book like* Praying with Beads: Daily Prayers for the Christian Year[8] *can guide you into restful prayer if you find that grief makes even connection with God difficult to sustain.*

A Song to Encourage Your Heart: *"Surrounded (Fight My Battles)" by Michael W. Smith*

Supportive relationships keep our heads above water when we feel like we're drowning in sorrow. They keep us walking toward new life when we'd rather sit by the side of the road and give up.

IT TAKES A VILLAGE

Praise be to the LORD, the God of Israel,
who has sent you today to meet me.

1 SAMUEL 25:32, NIV

Every year Hollywood awards ceremonies offer us a fascinating display of thankfulness. Celebrities walk across stages to celebrate their accomplishments, and as they stand in the spotlight alone, almost every famous actor or singer says the same thing: "I couldn't have done this without . . ." While fame and fortune may fall upon only a few, every artist knows that movies and music are collaborative ventures. Many helpers stand just beyond the stage light. They may not receive the applause, but they are indispensable to the art's success. To borrow a popular phrase, it takes a village to make a hit movie.

First Samuel 25 chronicles the story of David's conflict with Nabal. Nabal was a hothead landowner who insulted David, and David's first impulse was to fight back. Abigail, Nabal's wife, knew better, though. After years of living with her foolish husband, she understood that fighting fire with fire only resulted in everyone being burned. Instead, she wisely advised David toward peace, gently correcting and redirecting him. Her counsel convicted David of his sinful ambitions, saved people from bloodshed, and pointed David toward actions that would bring God glory instead of dishonor. Abigail knew it took a loving, truthtelling village to raise a king.

It takes a village to raise us, too, as we build new lives after loss. Contrary to the Western image of the cowboy riding the range alone, we were built for relationships, and we thrive when we enjoy their comfort, support, and encouragement. Supportive relationships keep our heads above water when we feel like we're drowning in sorrow. They keep us walking toward new life when we'd rather sit by the side of the road and give up. And they speak truth to us when we need to hear it most.

All of us need more than yes-men on our support teams. We need Abigails, too—those wise friends who can offer an honest, firm, corrective word that directs us toward new life. Like an artistic director in a movie or an Abigail in the desert, these supporters offer us important outside perspectives that can help us see more clearly. They aren't critical; they're corrective. They're not callous; they're caring. Today, thank God for your team of support, even the ones who deliver words that are sometimes hard to hear. Thanks be to God that it takes a village to raise a grieving person! He doesn't leave us to walk this hard road alone.

Though one may be overpowered, two can defend themselves.
A cord of three strands is not quickly broken.
ECCLESIASTES 4:12, NIV

These are the things you are to do: Speak the truth to each other, and render true and sound judgment in your courts.
ZECHARIAH 8:16, NIV

A Prayer: *God, I admit that I prefer to hear only encouraging words. I don't respond well to critique. I'm sensitive to being told I might be wrong. However, I know that you've placed friends in my life who speak true, hard, and honest words. Thank you for their presence, even when I don't want to hear what they have to say. Today, Lord, teach me to receive exhortation with a gracious spirit. Help me to see myself as others see me. Let my relationships be as iron sharpening iron, making me more like you. Amen.*

An Activity for Today: *Hopefully, you've had many folks help you since your person died. Friends have sent cards and meals. Family has offered emotional support. We need this circle of care to help us live and thrive again. But did you know that your participation in that circle of care can also boost your resilience? Research has shown that people who help others feel happier, their overall moods are more stable, and they experience a stronger sense of well-being. Today, extend some of the comfort you've received from the Lord through your circle of support. Help a friend with a task. Volunteer to sit in the yard and weed with your neighbor. Pick up your nephew from school as a help to your sibling. Make cookies for an elderly person in your church who has been laid up with illness. Grief can make our worlds feel very small, but compassion can open them up again. Ask God to help you see, through your acts of service, how big your world actually is.*

A Song to Encourage Your Heart: *"To Tell the Truth" by Sovereign Grace Music*

Grief isn't always simply

love with no place to

go. Sometimes saying

goodbye to our person

is complicated.

A NEW KIND
OF FORGIVENESS

How the mighty have fallen!
The weapons of war have perished!

2 SAMUEL 1:27, NIV

After Saul's death, David led Israel in formal mourning for the late king's passing. Saul's volatility, aggression, jealousy, and hatred had marked their relationship since David's adolescence, and you might imagine that David's first thought upon hearing of his death would be rejoicing. *Finally, no more running for my life. Finally, no more threats against my kingdom. Finally, peace after years of anxiety and hurt.* Who could mourn the death of a man who had been so unkind? Wasn't Saul's death the result of his own sinfulness anyway?

However, when David learned that Saul had died, he grieved—no doubt, a complicated grief of relief and sorrow for what was and could have been. And when it came time to publicly eulogize Saul, David found honest yet gracious words to bring peace to his nation.

In his eulogy, David describes Saul as swifter than an eagle and stronger than a lion, and we're reminded both of Saul's charismatic personality and his deft skill as he threw a spear at David in the royal court. When David laments that the mighty have fallen, we remember Saul's military skill and his dogged pursuit of David in caves and across the desert. David finds ways to be both honest and honoring as he says goodbye to this leader who shaped David's own destiny. More than simply mourning, David's honesty creates a path toward forgiveness, even when he can't experience reconciliation with Saul.

You may be surprised to realize you have many more feelings after your loss than sadness. If your friend became distant because of addiction, you may experience frustration or regret. If your loved one took his or her life, you may feel confused or angry. If your relationship with your parent or child was marked by tension or discord, you may feel relieved that you don't have to deal with those problems anymore. Grief isn't always simply love with no place to go. Sometimes saying goodbye to our person is complicated.

If that's you, consider how you can grieve with love and truth today. How can your honest words about your loss create a path for forgiveness? How can you extend grace to your person in his or her death and offer grace to yourself as you consider the many ways that relationship didn't meet your needs? Grieving a complicated relationship isn't easy, but God meets us even here with his promise of mercy and transforming grace.

An honest answer is like a kiss of friendship.
PROVERBS 24:26, NLT

You must not testify falsely against your neighbor.
EXODUS 20:16, NLT

A Prayer: *God, I wish my grief were less complicated. I wish this goodbye were easier. Please take all of my feelings and sort them out in your holiness. Convict me of sinful thoughts and words against my person. Teach me to be merciful. Reveal to me your grace extended to me, and help me to extend it to those who have hurt and disappointed me. Heal my side of the relationship, even though my person is no longer living, and give me peace. Amen.*

An Activity for Today: *For centuries, different flowers have held symbolic meanings and were gifted on specific occasions. Today, allow flowers to speak the words that you long to say to or about your person. Seek out stunning blooms in your neighborhood or grocery store and allow their fragrance, color, and shape to remind you of the beauty of your person's life. If your relationship with your person was hard, allow the blossoms to bring God's goodness, truth, and beauty to mind. If you can't get out to browse or buy, look at pictures online of a flower that symbolizes qualities you saw in your person. Visit The Old Farmer's Almanac online for a comprehensive list of flowers and their traditional meanings.*

A Song to Encourage Your Heart: *"There's a Wideness in God's Mercy" by St. Paul's Cathedral Choir*

The psalmist knows that

true rest comes from

someplace even deeper

than healthy bedtime

routines. Only God can

make us dwell in safety.

GO TO BED, SLEEPYHEAD

In peace I will both lie down and sleep; for you
alone, O LORD, make me dwell in safety.

PSALM 4:8, ESV

Recently, our family adopted a hamster to join our home's menagerie. Kurt, named for one of the von Trapp children in *The Sound of Music*, came to us at just thirty days old. He could fit into a half-cup measuring scoop.

The animal rescue instructed us to hold Kurt three times daily as a way to get to know each other. Unfortunately, he'd scamper away under a cardboard hiding spot when the cage door opened and burrow under his wheel when a hand reached down to pick him up. Kurt didn't want to be held at all!

Over time, Kurt settled into the thrice-daily practice of being held. Though he'd initially resist, once he was safely enclosed in someone's hands, he curled up into a little ball, closed his eyes, and fell asleep. Every single time, the warmth of the holder's hands calmed him, perhaps triggering memories of his mother's safety. Consistent, gentle care could prompt rest.

It almost goes without saying that grief affects our rest after we lose a loved one. Whether we experience unexpected sluggishness or wide-eyed sleepless nights, loss throws off our circadian rhythms and makes rest often hard to find. Moreover, the stressors of life after loss can compound our bodies' struggles for sleep.

We're deeply tired. But like little Kurt, we keep running on our wheels and running away from the things that can offer us true relief.

While we can't force our bodies to sleep, we can learn the habits of peaceful rest. A cooler room, no screens before bedtime, and meditative practices like prayer or mindful breathing can all prompt restfulness even when sleep feels hard to attain. Rest can become a goal all its own in grief.

However, the psalmist knows that true rest comes from someplace even deeper than healthy bedtime routines. Only God can make us dwell in safety—safety from our own whirling minds, safety from fears about tomorrow, safety from physical threats and loneliness. True rest comes from trust in God.

Today, as you find space for slowing down, receive that space and peace as a gift from God. Whether sleeping is easy or hard, God is with you in it, offering comfort and sustaining grace. You can both rest and sleep when the everlasting arms enfold you. Renewing sleep may take time to return after the death of your person, but it doesn't need to be elusive forever. As you rest in God, you can be assured he will give you exactly what you need.

I lie down and sleep; I wake again, because the Lord sustains me.
PSALM 3:5, NIV

You can go to bed without fear; you will lie down and sleep soundly. You need not be afraid of sudden disaster or the destruction that comes upon the wicked, for the Lord is your security.
PROVERBS 3:24-26, NLT

A Prayer: *God, good sleep has been hard to find since my person died. My body and mind struggle to relax. My fears creep in at nighttime. I take comfort that you never slumber or sleep. You are awake in the middle of the night, and you promise to hold me as I rest. Please help me commit to resting today as an act of trust. Please give me sleep today that renews me to face what you have placed before me. Amen.*

An Activity for Today: *Find some rest today using a technique that therapists call progressive relaxation. First, find a comfortable, quiet space to settle your body. Whether lying down or sitting with your feet gently settled on the floor, close your eyes and take a slow, cleansing breath. Next, starting with your toes, tense your muscles, hold for four counts, and release. Move from your toes to your calves to your thighs and all the way up your body as each part of you tenses, holds, and relaxes. Progressive relaxation helps you to identify parts of your body that are holding tension so that you can mindfully release it.*

A Song to Encourage Your Heart: *"All through the Night" by Tom Roush*

Learning to thrive again

after the death of a

loved one requires that we

make friends with grief's

darkness.

DARKNESS AND LIGHT

You have taken from me friend and neighbor—
darkness is my closest friend.

PSALM 88:18, NIV

"Hello darkness, my old friend," sing Paul Simon and Art Garfunkel in their song "The Sound of Silence." "I've come to talk with you again." Written as Simon reflected on the assassination of President John F. Kennedy, the song speaks to the quiet that settles in after deep loss. For those living through the 1960s, the song would become an anthem of grief as the nation continued to suffer the crippling losses of prominent figures over the next decade.

Both the psalmist and Simon and Garfunkel use the word "friend" to describe darkness. For a long time, I thought their word choice was tongue in cheek, sardonic, or despairing. However, since my own loss, I've learned that darkness can offer unique and necessary friendship as we learn to cope with the deaths of those we love. In darkness, we discover truths about the world and ourselves that only sorrow can show.

After your person dies, darkness descends on your life in a way you've never known it before. Everyday joys lose their luster. The future looks uncertain, and the past becomes painful to remember. Like a lunar eclipse, grief moves across the face of your life, blotting out the sun of happiness and contentment and peace. Like the psalmist, you look at your life and see only loss.

Learning to thrive again after the death of a loved one requires that we make friends with grief's darkness by turning to our tender places with self-compassion and grace. This means acknowledging that darkness exists after loss and facing that darkness honestly. We need not gloss over our pain or try to outrun it. Instead, we listen to our fears, anxieties, sadness, and frustration and receive the important information that darkness has to offer us. Darkness can teach us vital lessons about our priorities and values. Death and loss can show us truths about our characters, places for repentance and growth. Darkness may be an unlikely and unwelcome friend, but it is a valuable one nonetheless.

Christians can face grief's darkness without despairing because we are assured God is present with us in it. Psalm 139 tells us that there is no darkness too dark for God. To him, pitch-black midnight is the same as sunny high noon. When we turn to grief's darkness to learn its wisdom, we do so with a divine lamp to our feet and light to our path. On this road with sorrow, we walk hand in hand with grief and God.

Have you been running from grief's darkness, attempting to put on a cheerful face? Today, ask God to help you acknowledge the hard parts of your loss. You can face the darkness with confidence. The Light of Life illumines all your night.

———

You, LORD, are my lamp; the LORD turns my darkness into light.
2 SAMUEL 22:29, NIV

He reveals the deep things of darkness and brings utter darkness into the light.
JOB 12:22, NIV

A Prayer: *God, I confess that I don't want to look at the dark parts of my grief. I'd rather avoid than confront the deep pain of my loss. I don't want darkness to be my friend. But I know there are things you wish to teach me in this season that I could not learn any other way. Help me to turn to my grief and listen to its wisdom. Remind me that as I face my grief, I do not do it alone. You shine brightly in my darkness and fill my life with light. Amen.*

An Activity for Today: *Have people told you since your loss that you are strong or brave? You probably don't feel like you deserve the accolades when you know how weak or afraid you feel. Truly, though, you've done big things since your person died—big things worth celebrating.*

To mark all that you've accomplished, fill out the award on the next page. Identify something your person would be proud of if he or she could see you now. No win is too small to celebrate. Whether or not you feel it, you've done big things with God's help.

A Song to Encourage Your Heart: *"Christ, Be Our Light" by Bernadette Farrell*

CERTIFICATE OF ACHIEVEMENT

This award is presented to

_____

on this day

_____

for

David pours out his heart
to God with full-faced
honesty, knowing that God
cares, listens, and loves him
through everything he's
enduring.

GOD IS LISTENING

My life is poured out like water, and all my bones are out of joint. My heart is like wax, melting within me.

PSALM 22:14, NLT

There's a popular acronym to describe oversharing these days—TMI. Too. Much. Information. If you share about your gastrointestinal distress at the dinner table, TMI. If you start talking about the details of your latest bunion surgery during a friend's birthday party, TMI. If you mention you're grieving months after your person's death, TMI. Nobody wants to hear all that.

It doesn't take long after your person's death to realize that there are some folks who can hear your story and others who can't. Some friends are equipped to listen to the blow-by-blow account of orchestrating a funeral or closing credit card accounts. Others weary of the details. Some family members welcome your expressions of sadness. Others can't seem to handle any talk of grief. TMI. Too. Much. Information. It can be really tough to discover this reality after loss. Not every person in your life can walk with you through this hard time.

When David wrote Psalm 22, he was in a real state of TMI. He's struggling with low self-image (verse 6). He feels abandoned by his circle of support (verse 11). But it doesn't stop there. David rattles off a laundry list of personal ailments that would make dinner party guests cringe—body aches, weakness, dry mouth, unhealthy weight loss. We read David's complaints and feel for him. Yet this is a psalm written for worship, to be sung by the congregation to a tune called "Doe of the Dawn." Doesn't he know these things aren't polite to share in public? Too. Much. Information.

David's oversharing isn't to be pitied, however. Instead, it should be praised. While David's friends don't seem willing to listen to his plight anymore, God's ears are always open. David has selected the perfect audience to whom he can complain and vent. In perfect love, God can receive all that David needs to get off his chest. There's nothing David can say that will make God love him less. There's no struggle David can share that will make God embarrassed or cringey. Instead, David pours out his heart to God with full-faced honesty, knowing that God cares, listens, and loves him through everything he's enduring.

As you cope with your loss, you may find that friends shy away from the details you wish to share. It may sometimes be tough to find a listening ear, even when you have a great circle of support. As you learn where and how to share your story best, remember that God is one person to whom you can give all the details. He knows your grief and loss and desires your company. There's no such thing as too much information with God.

———

The LORD is near to all who call on him, to all who call on him in truth.
PSALM 145:18, NIV

You keep track of all my sorrows. You have collected all my tears in your bottle. You have recorded each one in your book.
PSALM 56:8, NLT

A Prayer: *God, sometimes I feel like nobody wants to hear from me anymore. They only want the happy me that used to be. They're weary of hearing the details of my loss. Thank you, God, that you never grow tired of hearing from me. Thank you for letting me weep, ask questions, and complain to you. Your faithful presence reminds me that I am never truly alone, even when it feels like I've got no one left to talk to. Encourage me today with your presence. Remind me that you're listening and you love me. Amen.*

An Activity for Today: *Grief can make you feel like you're the only one with your kind of sadness. However, while grief is unique, it's also universal. Through the beauty of the internet, we can connect with others who have experienced similar losses and find comfort and solidarity as we grieve and grow. Today, do an internet search to find a local or online community of grievers who are mourning similar losses to yours. Search according to who you are (sibling, friend, parent, etc.) or how your person died (suicide, Alzheimer's, cancer, etc.). The following are just a few examples of possible connection and support:*

- *SiblingGriefClub.com for bereaved adult siblings*
- *CompassionateFriends.org for families grieving the death of a child*
- *TheDinnerParty.org for twenty- and thirtysomethings who have lost a loved one*
- *ModernWidowsClub.com for widows*
- *RefugeWidowers.com for widowed men*

A Song to Encourage Your Heart: *"God Is Listening" by Gohar Almas*

If you've stood at the

graveside and wondered,

How can I live? you are

not alone.

LIFE WITHOUT YOU

*The king was shaken. He went up to the room over the gateway
and wept. As he went, he said: "O my son Absalom! My
son, my son Absalom! If only I had died instead of you."*

2 SAMUEL 18:33, NIV

It's the late 1990s, and I'm driving along an Ohio back road
flanked by cornfields. Country music star Trisha Yearwood blasts
out of the speakers. *How do I live without you? I want to know.
How do I breathe without you, if you ever go?* I'm only nineteen
years old, and I've never really been in love, but somehow, even
in that naivete, Trisha's words ring true. Someday, I'm pretty sure
I'll lose someone I love, and I'll know the pain of heartbreak.

Years later, I—and you—know the seriousness that comes
along with the lament "How do I live without you?" When a
person has become such a part of your orbit that their presence
helps you discern other bodies in motion, their departure—
whether anticipated or sudden—shakes your entire universe.
You're left floating without gravity, without a North Star.
Everything, even the air, changes. You're not sure you can keep
breathing.

Lest you think this description overly dramatic, King David
expressed just the same when he learned of his son Absalom's
death. David's third-born son had grown into a handsome, charismatic man, but he was troubled too. Absalom loved power,

and he stole the throne from his father, causing David to flee for safety. Theirs was a troubled relationship.

Yet upon hearing of Absalom's violent death, David mourned with agonizing passion. This son who had caused his father grief in life now did the same in death. The missed opportunities, the conflicts that could never be resolved, the hurt that would now walk with David to his own grave—all of these compounded David's sadness, leaving him despairing of life itself.

If you've stood at the graveside and wondered, *How can I live?* you are not alone. You are not alone in wishing that the clock's hands could be rewound, that this bad dream was one from which you could awaken. These are very human responses, the natural emotional markers of tragedy. The question for you today is, What will you do with these feelings? Will you ignore them and fill your life with busyness to anesthetize you from the pain? Will you wander deeper into grief's pain and despair of life itself? Or, with God's strong hand guiding you, will you face these hard feelings, sit with them in self-compassion, and cling to God for comfort and hope? God stands ready to support you as you grieve. How will you choose to live without your person?

My soul clings to you; your right hand upholds me.
PSALM 63:8, ESV

I cried out, "I am slipping!" but your unfailing love, O LORD, supported me. When doubts filled my mind, your comfort gave me renewed hope and cheer.
PSALM 94:18-19, NLT

A Prayer: *God, I don't know how to live without my person. We can't talk or text or call anymore. I can't see or touch my person's face. I've loved them so long, I don't know how to move about my day without their physical or emotional presence. Sometimes, like King David, I even wish that I had died instead of them. But I trust that you still have lots of life for me to live. Even though I don't see how I can survive, you will show me how. As I face this day, give me the strength and courage and hope to live. Remind me that even when my feelings are very big, you are bigger. You will bring me from surviving to thriving again. Amen.*

An Activity for Today: *The theory of continuing bonds tells us that bereaved people thrive when they are able to bring their person into the lives they live without them. For many people, this means engaging with a cause that was important to their loved one. Today, consider making a donation to an organization that mattered to your person. Donate cat food to your local animal shelter. Sign up to run a 5K with one of her favorite nonprofits. Give a gift in your person's name to honor his or her legacy. While no act of charity can bring our person back to us, we can celebrate our loved one's life as we invest in things that matter. In doing so, we honor his or her life and can bring new purpose to our own in the process.*

A Song to Encourage Your Heart: *"Awake My Soul" by Chris Tomlin (featuring Lecrae)*

God wired us for resilience

and built us for resurrection.

Hope is woven into our DNA.

A TIME TO BUILD

*[David] said to Nathan the prophet, "Here I am, living
in a house of cedar, while the ark of God remains in a
tent." Nathan replied to the king, "Whatever you have in
mind, go ahead and do it, for the LORD is with you."*

2 SAMUEL 7:2-3, NIV

Over the last twenty years, HGTV—Home & Garden
Television—has brought new fascination to home design. From
shows about large-scale renovations to programming with do-it-
yourself possibilities, we've become obsessed with constructing
and feathering our nests. It's hardly any surprise. We are made in
God's image to be fixers and builders and lovers of beauty.

After worshiping in a temporary sanctuary for generations,
Israel needed a permanent place to worship God. King David
knew the longing that came with always being on the move,
and he craved a space where he could honor God with beautiful
craftsmanship, fragrant offerings, and awe-inspiring worship. So
as he aged, David consulted his good friend, the prophet Nathan,
about building plans.

However, David's timeline didn't match what God had in
mind. Nathan approved moving forward. However, when David
approached the Lord to propose his plan, God stopped him in
his tracks. "It's not time yet," God told David, much to his disappointment and dismay. He could gather the supplies, God said,

but no building should begin. Instead, someday, David's son Solomon would oversee that project.

David's heart was in the right place, but his timing was wrong. The Master Builder had a different construction plan in mind. For now, God intended to build *within* David and Israel instead. God's design was to form his people into a nation of peace and faithfulness whose legacy would last forever. Physical building projects could wait until later. There was other work to do.

In grief, so many rebuilding projects call out for our attention. Sometimes the list looks daunting, and we freeze, overwhelmed. Other times, though, the dizzying array of tasks can drive us to frenzied work. We chase after progress as confirmation that we're making it through the valley of the shadow.

There is certainly a time to build after loss. God wired us for resilience and built us for resurrection. Hope is woven into our DNA. But if you've felt the stress and strain to rebuild since your person died, you can take heart alongside King David today. Even with the greatest plans, today may not be the day to start.

Instead of fretting, bring your building projects to God and ask him to guide you into what you should do next. Is it time to gather up the supplies you'll need to rebuild—added sleep, nourishing meals, fortified friendships? Is it time to rest because God assures you that the work will be shared by others? Today, in the chaos that accompanies your loss, take a moment and hand your blueprints to God. He promises to make everything beautiful in his own time.

Unless the LORD builds the house, the builders labor in vain. Unless the LORD watches over the city, the guards stand watch in vain.

PSALM 127:1, NIV

I will give you thanks, for you answered me; you have become my salvation. The stone the builders rejected has become the cornerstone; the LORD has done this, and it is marvelous in our eyes.

PSALM 118:21-23, NIV

A Prayer: Lord Jesus, you are the cornerstone on which I find security. Even while I grieve and life feels uncertain, thank you that I can rest firm in you. Forgive me for giving in to the temptation of constructing my life apart from you. Teach me to follow you closely and surrender my plans to you. Show me the goodness of your intentions for me, and help me to trust that you hold all things in your control. Amen.

An Activity for Today: Are you frustrated about life's uncertainties? Do you wish you had a clearer timeline? You may have some anger you need to face as you acknowledge these disappointments. On the lines below, brainstorm three things you can do when you feel upset, frustrated, or angry. As you write your list, consider how these activities can help you identify your feelings honestly, engage them, and move through them with productive action. God understands that you're living in the in-between right now. It's okay to feel big feelings. You show that you trust him every time you face your emotions and offer them to him.

_____

_____

_____

_____

_____

_____

_____

A Song to Encourage Your Heart: "Your Plans for Us" by Eleventh Hour Worship

God is not offended by the

widow's despair. God receives

her just as she is. No polite

facade necessary.

GOD OF THE ELEVENTH HOUR

This is what the LORD, the God of Israel, says: "The jar of flour will not be used up and the jug of oil will not run dry until the day the LORD sends rain on the land."

1 KINGS 17:14, NIV

You've probably heard stories like this before. A waitress who is late on her rent receives an extra generous tip that covers the difference between her account balance and what's needed. A dad who's lost his job arrives home from another fruitless day of pounding the pavement for work to find a bag of groceries on his front stoop. We hear these stories and marvel. "Miracles still can happen," we say.

When you're grieving, however, it can be hard to hear other people's stories of miraculous provision. You prayed just as fervently as they did, but a cure never came. You trusted that God would provide, but it appears he answered no to your request. In the case of today's Scripture—why do some widows get jars of flour and oil while others go hungry? How can a story of one woman's amazing gift encourage us when we know that sometimes God doesn't show up in the ways we'd hoped?

The story of Elijah and the widow of Zarephath not only reminds us that God will meet our needs; it also invites us into a relationship with God that is deeper and rawer than any we may have known before. When Elijah visits the widow, she tells him plainly that she's past the eleventh hour of suffering. No husband. No food. No hope. She'll gather some firewood, she says, and head home to die alongside her son. The widow does not feign belief or measure her words. She doesn't even mention God. How could he be helpful at this point anyway?

As we grieve with honesty before God, this "before" part of the widow's story is just as important as what comes after. God is not offended by the widow's despair. He doesn't chastise her for her lack of faith in miracles. Instead, God receives her just as she is. No polite facade necessary.

What is the miracle in the story of Elijah and the widow? Yes, it's the oil and flour that don't run out. Even more, it is the tender, faithful God who welcomes us no matter if our faith is large or small. When belief runs thin and despair sets in, he doesn't leave us. Whatever the results of our prayers, today receive this intimate connection as a miracle worthy of praise in your grief.

———

I am the LORD your God, who brought you up out of Egypt. Open wide your mouth and I will fill it.
PSALM 81:10, NIV

The LORD Almighty is with us; the God of Jacob is our fortress.
PSALM 46:7, NIV

A Prayer: God, I wish you always answered my prayers the way I want them answered. I don't understand why you sometimes seem silent. I don't know why you sometimes seem to say no. I hear other people's miracle stories, and I jealously want my own. Help me to remember that the miracle is not in what you provide but in who you are to me, my Savior and Lord. You've chosen me and love me with an everlasting love. You are all-wise and all-knowing; nothing that concerns me is beyond your notice. Teach me to enjoy the miracle of our relationship today. Amen.

An Activity for Today: Take a gentle trip down memory lane by breaking out a photo album and mindfully journeying through the pictures today. (If you haven't made a scrapbook or photo album, perhaps today is a prompt to start that project!)

As you look through photographs, don't rush. Approach them like an investigator, carefully observing small details. Who is in the foreground? Look at facial expressions and bodily postures. Make note of clothing and accessories. Let these details draw forth memories. Sit compassionately with them and take your time.

Next, start to look beyond the subjects of the photographs to the context. What do you notice? If you're also in the pictures, allow your mind to drift back to that time. What stands out to you as you remember? Thank God for the life of your person and the treasure that these tangible memories hold. With each photograph, thank God that he is the unseen presence in every one. There is no moment he has ever been absent from your life or your loved one's life.

A Song to Encourage Your Heart: "Near the Cross" by The Petersens

When the chaos of those

first days and weeks dies

down, God's voice still

reassures you of his love

and presence.

DO YOU HEAR WHAT I HEAR?

After the earthquake there was a fire, but the LORD was not in the fire. And after the fire there was the sound of a gentle whisper.

1 KINGS 19:12, NLT

Did you know that dogs can hear so well that they can sometimes predict earthquakes? God designed dogs' ears with sensitivities that far surpass their human owners'. Not only can they hear lower and higher frequencies than we can, but dogs can also detect sounds that travel from far away—sometimes deep below the ground. What might sound to us like a whisper—or no sound at all!— can come through loud and clear to our canine friends.

Many people say that during the most acute part of their experience with loss—at the deathbed, during the funeral service—they feel God near. Prayers rise from family and friends on their behalf, and they sense they are held and carried by the intercessions of others. They may feel God speaking words of peace or hope or comfort in those darkest hours.

But as the dust settles and the casseroles stop arriving and the visitors wind down, God seems to get quiet too. Is he tired from exerting himself so much at the memorial service? Has he moved on to other emergency rooms and other deathbeds? That clarion voice that once guided us when death loomed large now grows almost imperceivable. Where is God, and what is he doing?

The prophet Elijah wondered much the same thing when

he ran away to the desert. He'd seen God work mightily: feeding him with ravens, sustaining the widow of Zarephath, and raining down fire on his offerings in a contest with the pagan prophets of Baal. Nevertheless, as trouble dragged on, Elijah began to wonder if God was even still paying attention. "I'm the only one left," he complained to God as he hid from his enemies. It was getting awfully quiet and lonesome.

Into that silence God brought drama and noise, but to Elijah's surprise, God's presence was not in these. Instead, God made himself known to Elijah in a whisper, an intimate sound so faint only a heart attuned like Elijah's could hear. God knew just how to talk with Elijah in his weariness and discouragement. Elijah thought he needed thunder; God knew he needed quiet.

God knows how to talk to you in your weariness too. When the chaos of those first days and weeks dies down, God's voice still reassures you of his love and presence. He may not speak in clapping thunder in this season, but he is still with you. As you grieve and learn to live without your person, receive God in quietness, a sound that with mindful attention your heart can hear.

I will lead her into the desert and speak tenderly to her there. I will return her vineyards to her and transform the Valley of Trouble into a gateway of hope.
HOSEA 2:14-15, NLT

"LORD, help!" they cried in their trouble, and he saved them from their distress. He calmed the storm to a whisper and stilled the waves. What a blessing was that stillness as he brought them safely into harbor!
PSALM 107:28-30, NLT

A Prayer: *God, I long to hear your voice like I did around the time of my person's death. You felt so close, and your comfort seemed so clear. Now, tiredness wears me down and life moves on, and I don't notice you in the same ways that I did before. By your Spirit, tune my ears to hear your voice. Sharpen my attention so that I notice your movement in my life. Refresh me with your promises and remind me that even when the intensity of my loss ebbs away, you are still here beside me, speaking words of comfort and hope. Amen.*

An Activity for Today: *God created your body with amazing attention to detail, and your body is always sending you messages. Where do you feel your grief today? Sit for a moment in silence and close your eyes. Scan your body from head to toe and gently identify places of tension, ache, or pain. As you do, take a deep breath in, hold it for four counts, and exhale, imagining that you are blowing the discomfort out of that space of your body. Mark on the diagram of the person below where you feel your grief today so that you can go back and see how it shifts from day to day.*

A Song to Encourage Your Heart: *"Those Who Have Not Seen" by Anchor Hymns*

As you sit by your own rivers

of Babylon, remember that

there's no such thing as

the good old days. Even here

in grief's foreign land, you

are not exiled from God's

goodness.

LOOKING BACK AND LOOKING FORWARD

*By the rivers of Babylon we sat and
wept when we remembered Zion.*

PSALM 137:1, NIV

The famous American satirist Peter De Vries once quipped, "Nostalgia ain't what it used to be." Ain't it the truth! While many people look to the past with warm remembrance, bereaved people can't do that as easily. We know how the story ends. We know that every happy memory stands on a time line that leads toward death. Nostalgia doesn't make us smile; it pinches.

Try as we might, looking back at the good old days rarely brings the comforting feelings we hope it will. Instead, it often produces disillusionment, disappointment, and lingering sadness. Our reflections on the past tend to highlight the good and diminish the bad. We can clearly see God's goodness in the rearview mirror, but what is he doing now in our grief? Nostalgia offers a dangerous temptation to rewrite the past as the only place of God's favor.

As the Jews sat beside the rivers of Babylon, they cried when they remembered the good old days. Nostalgia for the familiar blurred the reality of what their life had really been like. The people reminisced about Jerusalem as their "highest joy"

(Psalm 137:6), while in truth the nation had wandered far from the Lord. They lived in an exile of their own making, a result of their sin. Only when the past was no longer accessible did it become so sweet.

It's normal to struggle with nostalgia as you grieve the death of your loved one. Reflecting on our pasts is an important part of grieving and growing, and you should carve out space to engage in this thoughtfully. However, as you sit by your own rivers of Babylon, remember that there's no such thing as the good old days. Even here in grief's foreign land, you are not exiled from God's goodness. The same God who wrote your past is writing your story today. He holds your past, present, and future in his loving hands. You do not ever live a day apart from his goodness.

Just as we must offer God our futures, we must give to him our pasts as well. You can hand God your rose-colored glasses and look at your past honestly. You can release your nostalgia and receive God's presence in your present. Today, take this first step to embrace your hard story as the rich soil in which your new life after loss can grow.

You will show faithfulness to Jacob and steadfast love to Abraham, as you have sworn to our fathers from the days of old.
MICAH 7:20, ESV

He is the Rock; his deeds are perfect. Everything he does is just and fair. He is a faithful God who does no wrong; how just and upright he is!
DEUTERONOMY 32:4, NLT

A Prayer: Dear God, when I look back at my life before loss, everything seems better. I know life wasn't perfect, but at least my person was alive. It's hard for me to be honest sometimes about what life really was like before death came into it. Today, God, help me to tell the truth about my past. As I weep for what was, give me clarity to acknowledge what was true about the life I lived before. And in this truth, ground me as I step into this day. Show me that each day is full of your new mercies. Give me grace and courage to receive them. Amen.

An Activity for Today: Grief researchers Margaret Stroebe and Henk Schut developed what they called a dual process model of coping with bereavement. Stroebe and Schut studied bereaved people and saw that the ones who learn to thrive again move back and forth between loss- and restoration-oriented behaviors. They lean into grief and then let go. They rest in acknowledgment of their hard emotions and also learn to push through them like seedlings through soil toward new life. This "oscillation," said Stroebe and Schut, is a necessary part of developing the muscles for life after loss.

On the next page is the diagram of loss- and restoration-oriented behaviors that Stroebe and Schut developed to illustrate this movement in grief.[9] Fill in each section of the diagram with your own experiences of loss- and restoration-oriented activity. Where do you notice that you need to lean into your grief and feel its weight? Where do you see God calling you to expand your vision of your life after loss? As you fill in the diagram, remember: there is no wrong or right here. Each activity is a natural part of rebuilding after loss. Let this activity help you chart the resilience God is developing inside of you.

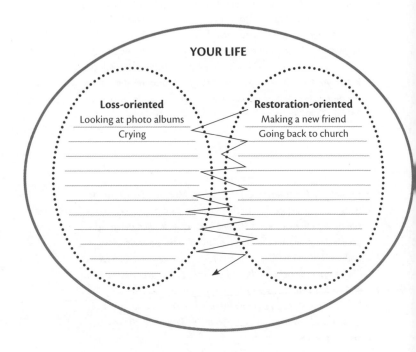

YOUR LIFE

Loss-oriented
Looking at photo albums
Crying

Restoration-oriented
Making a new friend
Going back to church

A Song to Encourage Your Heart: "Great Is Thy Faithfulness" by Austin Stone Worship

God promises to restore

your life in his good time,

but he wants you to be

a colaborer with him

in the process.

WHAT CAN YOU MAKE WITH THAT?

*I will bring Judah and Israel back from captivity
and will rebuild them as they were before.*

JEREMIAH 33:7, NIV

After almost two decades of parenting, I've learned that there are two different kinds of LEGO kids. One LEGO builder opens the box and follows the instructions to build a structure that will sit on a bookshelf or desk for display. The other LEGO builder does the same, only he or she has no illusions of permanence. When a new creative idea strikes, the structure undergoes dismantling. Bricks used to build a Millennium Falcon combine with pieces from a LEGO Friends pet hotel, and a totally new idea emerges. There's no set of instructions for this one. The end result is entirely in the mind of the creator.

As the Israelites sat in Babylonian exile, Jerusalem's destruction left them with few illusions of rebuilding. Even if they could get home to their ancestral lands, the task of sorting out the rubble and starting new would be daunting. Like taking pieces from one LEGO structure and snapping them onto another, rebuilding efforts would require painstaking care and a fresh sense of creativity. What could you make with the mess of the life you'd lived before?

As God met with Jeremiah, he didn't give him all the details of how Israel's restoration would take place. Jeremiah and Israel would need to trust God's wisdom and vision like they'd never done before. They'd need to stick close to him, keep talking to him, and recommit their lives to him if rebuilding would ever be successful. "Call to me," God told Jeremiah, "and I will answer you and tell you great and unsearchable things you do not know" (Jeremiah 33:3, NIV). As the Israelites did this, like a good LEGO manual, God would give step-by-step instructions on how to move forward. One step at a time. Enough for today. Rebuilding slowly, piece by piece.

Perhaps you feel similarly bewildered as you look at the pieces of the life that death broke apart. There's no set of instructions on how to build this life after loss, and frankly you're too tired or sad or foggy most of the time to even try to create a back-of-the-napkin alternative plan. This is a life you didn't anticipate, and you're not sure where to start. You can't even envision what God might have in mind for you next.

Today, receive both the promise of God and the encouragement of God for your own rebuilding task. God promises to restore your life in his good time, but he wants you to be a colaborer with him in the process. What's your job? Keep talking to him and ready your heart to work when he calls you to your next task.

———

Your word is a lamp to my feet and a light to my path.
PSALM 119:105, ESV

Guide me in your truth and teach me, for you are God my Savior, and my hope is in you all day long.
PSALM 25:5, NIV

A Prayer: God, you have promised that when I call upon you, you will answer me. Today, I need a hope that only you can offer. I know that you desire my flourishing, but I'm not sure how to get there. Your thoughts and plans are higher and better than any I could imagine. Infuse my heart with hope as you show me what you have for me to do today. I am open to your simple instructions. I am willing to take this one step at a time. You will make everything beautiful in its time. Amen.

An Activity for Today: Imagine that your person could bestow upon you a gift from his or her personality. What do you think you would receive? Would Mom give you her common sense? Would your cousin offer you his gift of gab? Select an aspect of your person's personality and receive it as a gift today. Purpose to emulate this quality of your person as you go to work, interact with your family, or hang out with friends. Let your imitation of your loved one celebrate his or her life continuing on in you.

A Song to Encourage Your Heart: "If the Lord Builds the House" by Hope Darst

In his resurrection, he unlocked

the possibility of resurrection

in our lives too.

YOU'VE GOT HIS FACE

I'll reward him extravagantly—the best of everything, the highest honors—because he looked death in the face and didn't flinch, because he embraced the company of the lowest.

ISAIAH 53:12, MSG

Over the years since my husband's death, I've marveled to see his attributes emerge in our children. One child mirrors his quiet steadiness; another has his knack for fixing things. It brings me joy to see the many ways that my husband lives in those he loved most.

After we lose a loved one, we often go looking for his or her attributes in ourselves or those around us. We encourage a friend with "You've got your mother's eyes" as she grieves the death of her beloved parent. We remind a colleague that she's got her sister's wit or his best friend's knack for hospitality. These resemblances can give us courage or comfort as we rebuild our lives after loss. They anchor us in those relationships that must now live on in our memories.

As Israel waited in captivity for rescue, Isaiah prophesied that a Savior would come who looked like them. They were stuck in a mess from which they couldn't escape, but a Messiah would arrive who both deserved the greatest honor and would endure the deepest pain. He'd keep company with the lowest because he had chosen to be like them in every way. Israel's entire hope rested on this promise. One day, their rescuer would be both "Mighty God" and a man "acquainted with grief" (Isaiah 9:6; 53:3, ESV).

Many years later, the New Testament writer of Hebrews recalled these promises given to Isaiah and connected them to the man Jesus. Jesus was the fulfillment of this promise, the writer asserted, the one made like us in order that we could be made like him. Jesus knew what it was like to face dying. He knew what it was like to grieve. And most glorious of all, Jesus knew what it meant to rise again. Through his death on the cross for our sins and his resurrection from the grave, Jesus would fulfill all of Israel's longings for freedom—and all of ours. In his resurrection, he unlocked the possibility of resurrection in our lives too.

Jesus walks beside us through grief, not as one who has a head knowledge of loss but as one who understands it in every corner of his being. His restored humanity offers us a glimpse of the new life we can live after loss. Today, rejoice that Isaiah's prophecy has been fulfilled. Hallelujah, Jesus came to take on our face and take our place!

For to us a child is born, to us a son is given, and the government will be on his shoulders. And he will be called Wonderful Counselor, Mighty God, Everlasting Father, Prince of Peace.
ISAIAH 9:6, NIV

Fear not, for I have redeemed you; I have called you by name, you are mine.
ISAIAH 43:1, ESV

A Prayer: God, I praise and thank you for your great plan of salvation. Thank you for coming in Jesus to become like me in every way. Thank you for understanding my pain and lifting me to new life through your resurrection. When I feel isolated, help me to remember that you understand every part of what it means to be human. Refresh me with the truth that you know what my life is like. Empower me to live for you, bearing your face to those I meet. Amen.

An Activity for Today: Psalm 145 instructed Israel to tell God's wondrous acts from one generation to another. God's people were to be storytellers and story-keepers, introducing him to those who would never see the Red Sea split or find manna outside their tents.

You can be a storyteller and story-keeper too. Today, be the curator of your relationship and share about it with someone who didn't know your person. Over lunch with a colleague, weave in a funny story about Grandpa. On the car ride home from school, tell your kids stories of Mom's culinary exploits, extravagant meals she made when they were only eating baby food. When we tell stories, we remember that grief is more than just sadness. It is a multifaceted experience that can include joy, respect, and sweetness also.

A Song to Encourage Your Heart: "There Was Jesus" by Zach Williams and Dolly Parton

The life you lived before

your loss can become the

fertile nursery from which a

beautiful future can grow.

DAY 38

NEW FROM OLD

*In that day the Root of Jesse will stand as a banner
for the peoples; the nations will rally to him,
and his resting place will be glorious.*

ISAIAH 11:10, NIV

On the Pieropan Christmas Tree Farm in western Massachusetts, Emmet Van Driesche grows all of his trees from stumps using a technique called coppicing. As trees age, they are cut at the base, their still-alive stumps becoming the nursery where multiple new shoots can grow. For millennia, farmers have used this technique to produce more wood faster, to maximize limited space, and to open the forest floor and bring sunlight to new growth.

When Isaiah prophesied about the coming Messiah, he used this picture of coppicing—a root springing from the stump of Jesse, new growth from something others might have considered dead. This Messiah would restore Israel's hopes for the future and remind them that God's promises were still alive if they would wholeheartedly obey. The shoot from the stump of Jesse would rise tall like a banner, drawing his people to himself—a rallying cry like the kind that heralded men for battle. However, this tall, beautiful shoot would not call nations to war but to peace. As they gathered under the shade of this new coppiced growth, Israel would find rest.

As you look at the stump of your own life, it may be hard

159

to believe that anything could grow out of it again. Like Israel, you may wonder if salvation from your bleak situation will ever come. You've been cut off at the roots, severed by death from the life you loved before. What good could grow in your life now? You know you must go on, but you're not sure you see hope or purpose in your future.

God's promise of the Root of Jesse offers you hope today. Just like that coppiced tree growing out of Israel's broken stump, God will raise up new life in you. The life you lived before your loss can become the fertile nursery from which a beautiful future can grow. You can draw from the nutrients of your past—your deep love for your person and the lessons you learned from life together—and find nourishment in Christ, the Light of Life (see John 1:4). God will grow your life again as you root yourself in him (see John 15:5).

Today, consider that what was "cut down" in your life can become the birthplace of new growth. The new life born from your grief can rise up like a beautiful new tree in the forest, your own rallying cry, drawing others to hope in God. Your coppiced tree can become a resting place where God meets and intimately nourishes you for the future he has prepared for you.

The LORD replied, "My Presence will go with you, and I will give you rest."
EXODUS 33:14, NIV

The eternal God is your refuge, and his everlasting arms are under you.
DEUTERONOMY 33:27, NLT

A Prayer: *Dear God, you are making all things new, and this includes me. Help me to believe that you are growing something beautiful out of the stump of my old life. Nourish me with your presence, and sustain me as I experience the growth pains that come with starting over. Remind me to always turn to you as my source of life. Amen.*

An Activity for Today: *Many grieving people find comfort in owning something that belonged to their loved one, particularly a piece of clothing. There's something very intimate about being able to hold something that used to be so close to your person's body. Today, if you have a piece of your person's clothing, bring it out to hold and smell and caress. Wear it if it brings you comfort and peace. If you don't have a piece of clothing from your person, choose an outfit today that highlights one of his or her favorite colors or accessories. Wear a baseball cap in memory of Dad. Pull out your red sweater to honor your best friend's love of vibrant hues. Clothing can reflect how we feel inside. What you wear today can offer silent witness to your grief and love and reflect your person quietly to the world.*

A Song to Encourage Your Heart: *"Abide" by Jonni Mae*

Isaiah reminds Israel—

and us—that this hope

isn't just conjecture. God

has a clear plan in mind,

and he's already working

toward its fulfillment.

PHOTOS OF THE FUTURE

He will destroy the shroud that enfolds all peoples, the sheet
that covers all nations; he will swallow up death forever.
The Sovereign LORD will wipe away the tears from all faces;
he will remove his people's disgrace from all the earth.

ISAIAH 25:7-8, NIV

Social media loves photo manipulation, and so do I. I especially
love the apps that age a person's face so that you can imagine
them years older. While I don't ever wish for the years to actually
fly by, it's fun to imagine my kids as grandparents one day and to
see a computer's rendering of what they might look like. When
I see their wizened brows and gray hair, I have to smile. God
willing, there's so much life ahead for my children to enjoy.

While I can envision those things for my own children,
sometimes I find it more difficult to cast such a hopeful vision
for myself. Middle-aged and widowed, I realize my finitude more
than I'd like. Looking to the future means aging without my
sweet husband, finding fulfillment in ways I'd never planned or
imagined. I can plan more than I used to in early grief, but I still
can't see far ahead. Some days I'm not sure the future is as bright
for me as it is for my children.

I know I'm not alone in this struggle. I've talked to so many
grieving folks that I know you've probably felt this way too.
Maybe you woke up this morning in the middle of this particular
struggle for hope. When you "manipulate" the image you have

of yourself now, you see things that make you feel discouraged or anxious. You're not sure you like the picture of the future you see.

While Israel waited in exile, Isaiah painted many pictures to offer them hope. But no matter how many prophecies Isaiah delivered, Israel's fears still rested right beneath the surface. What would their future actually look like? And was it something they'd want when they got there? So under the Spirit's influence, Isaiah envisioned for Israel what their future would be.

Isaiah's prophecy was just a glimpse to get them dreaming, a foretaste to get them hungry. As in a photo app, the picture of Israel's current existence morphed into an image of abundance, life, joy, and freedom. The true future would be bigger, better, and brighter than anything they could imagine. No more death, no more tears, no more disgrace. All things new.

While grief requires that we attend to the very mundane parts of our physical, here-and-now lives, as Christians we are called to grieve *with hope* (see 1 Thessalonians 4:13). Isaiah reminds Israel—and us—that this hope isn't just conjecture. God has a clear plan in mind, and he's already working toward its fulfillment. One day, all of creation will be restored. Heaven will come down to earth. King Jesus will reign in glory and love. Today, fix your mind on heaven. Fast-forward for a bit and enjoy the picture of what will be.

———

Those who sow with tears will reap with songs of joy.
PSALM 126:5, NIV

Behold, I am doing a new thing; now it springs forth, do you not perceive it? I will make a way in the wilderness and rivers in the desert.
ISAIAH 43:19, ESV

A Prayer: God, I believe the promise of Isaiah that you will return to right every wrong and conquer death forever. How I long for that day! As I move about my work this day, remind me that heaven's glory awaits me. Train my heart to hope for what is to come, and encourage me to live like your promises are true. I can't wait to see you face-to-face. Amen.

An Activity for Today: The ancient Indians and Greeks had a proverb that said, "Blessed is the man who plants a tree whose shade he will never sit under." Today, enact your trust and plant a tree. Research an organization like the Arbor Day Foundation, a global nonprofit that fights deforestation, or a local nonprofit that works to plant native species in your area. Give a dollar, give an hour to weed out invasive species—whatever you can. Invest in something you'll never see grow to maturity because—even when it doesn't feel like it—this life is more than today. Let God's mighty oaks give you hope. There's growth ahead for you too.

A Song to Encourage Your Heart: "We Will Feast in the House of Zion" by Sandra McCracken

As you move and live
with grief, as you "start
back home" toward a
new life after loss,
God invites you to seize
eternity too.

CARPE AETERNUM

*They will ask the way to Jerusalem and will start back
home again. They will bind themselves to the LORD with
an eternal covenant that will never be forgotten.*

JEREMIAH 50:5, NLT

Before your person died, you may have engaged in conversations
about your mortality with a sense of glibness. When a friend
asked, "What would you want to do if you knew you'd die
tomorrow?" you could think of a laundry list to fill the time—
Starbucks with a friend, a trip to Venice, a ride on the world's
largest roller coaster. Chances are, the items that filled your imaginary bucket list were a mix of the mundane and the extraordinary. If you knew your time was short, you'd want to make the
most of it. You'd want to fill the moments with love and warmth
and thrills and delight. You'd want to *carpe diem*, seize the day.

Now that you live with grief, you may not like entertaining
thoughts of your own mortality. You've seen what it looks like
to have a loved one granted a finite amount of time. You've had
to wrestle with how to help your person spend their last days or
hours. You know that the idea of seizing the day, while exciting,
can sometimes be engulfed in life's harder realities. To give you
energizing hope in grief, you need something more than seizing
the day.

After the people of Judah were in Babylonian exile for many

years, God anointed Jeremiah to prophesy about the rebuilding of Jerusalem. For those who had wept when they remembered Zion (see Psalm 137:1), Jeremiah's news brought a thrill of hope. After so much sorrow in exile, the moment Israel longed for was finally approaching. When, years later, Nehemiah guided Israel in the rebuilding of Jerusalem's wall, the people worked with vigor to realize their long-held dreams. This was the moment, their finest hour! Or was it?

Years before Israel's dream was ever realized, Jeremiah knew that while seizing the day might give the people initial energy for the tasks that faced them, they'd need a stronger power for the long haul. Rather than fix their eyes only on what lay before them, the people would need to bind themselves to God with an everlasting covenant. They'd need to live with eternity in mind. This perspective would undergird them on days when their *carpe diem* energy kicked in. It would also sustain them on days when the task seemed long and monotonous. To live fully again, Israel would need to grasp hold of and delight in God's eternal plan for them. They'd need to *carpe aeternum*—seize eternity—instead.

As you move and live with grief, as you "start back home" toward a new life after loss, God invites you to seize eternity too. Yes, learn to take pleasure in this day and all it offers. But more than that, cling to the reality that these "light and momentary troubles are achieving for us an eternal glory that far outweighs them all" (2 Corinthians 4:17, NIV). You can live with grief and thrive after loss because God has bound himself to you in love, an eternal covenant that fuels your work today and will carry you forward into the good future he has planned for you.

Do you think I'd withdraw my holy promise? or take back words I'd already spoken? I've given my word, my whole and holy word.

PSALM 89:34-35, MSG

He was given authority, glory and sovereign power; all nations and peoples of every language worshiped him. His dominion is an everlasting dominion that will not pass away, and his kingdom is one that will never be destroyed.

DANIEL 7:14, NIV

A Prayer: *God, I want more than to live for today. Teach me to seize eternity and live with your greater purpose in mind. As I rebuild my life, show me how to invest in the work you have laid before me with a mindset marked by hope. Give me grace when I doubt; give me comfort when I am discouraged. You rebuild Israel's walls, and you'll rebuild my life. Give me confidence to live like I believe this. Amen.*

An Activity for Today: *You've traveled through forty days of remembrance. On this final day, use the space below to write a letter to your person. Allow the format to give voice to the things you need to say. Invite God to speak to your heart as you put words to the emotions you hold around your loss. Thank him for walking beside you through grief toward joy.*

- *I'm sorry . . .*
- *I forgive you . . .*
- *I want you to know . . .*
- *I love you . . .*

_____

_____

_____

_____

_____

_____

_____

_____

_____

_____

_____

_____
_____
_____
_____
_____
_____
_____
_____
_____
_____
_____
_____
_____
_____
_____
_____
_____
_____
_____
_____
_____
_____
_____
_____
_____

A Song to Encourage Your Heart: "Father, Let Your Kingdom Come" by The Porter's Gate

Notes

1. Dexter Louie, Karolina Brook, and Elizabeth Frates, "The Laughter Prescription: A Tool for Lifestyle Medicine," *American Journal of Lifestyle Medicine* 10, no. 4 (July–August 2016), https://www.ncbi.nlm.nih.gov/pmc/articles/PMC6125057/.
2. "Laughter-Based Exercise Program for Older Adults Has Health Benefits, Georgia State Researchers Find," Georgia State University, Georgia State News Hub, September 15, 2016, https://news.gsu.edu/2016/09/15/laughter-based-exercise-program-health-benefits-georgia-state-researchers-find/.
3. Aljoscha Dreisoerner et al., "Self-Soothing Touch and Being Hugged Reduce Cortisol Responses to Stress: A Randomized Controlled Trial on Stress, Physical Touch, and Social Identity," *Comprehensive Psychoneuroendocrinology*, October 8, 2021, https://www.ncbi.nlm.nih.gov/pmc/articles/PMC9216399/.
4. Alisha Coleman-Jensen et al., "Household Food Security in the United States in 2021," USDA Economic Research Service, September 2022, https://www.ers.usda.gov/publications/pub-details/?pubid=104655.
5. Thomas Merton, *Dialogues with Silence: Prayers and Drawings*, ed. Jonathan Montaldo (San Francisco: HarperSanFrancisco, 2004).
6. See Hafthor Bjornsson perform his record-breaking lift here: "Game of Thrones 'Mountain' Hafthor Bjornsson Breaks World Deadlift Record—Video," *Guardian*, May 3, 2020, https://www.theguardian.com/sport/video/2020/may/03/game-of-thrones-mountain-hafthor-bjornsson-breaks-world-deadlift-record-video.
7. Robert A. Johnson, *The Fisher King and the Handless Maiden:*

    Understanding the Wounded Feeling Function in Masculine and Feminine Psychology (San Francisco: HarperSanFrancisco, 1995), 6.

8. Nan Lewis Doerr and Virginia Stem Owens, *Praying with Beads: Daily Prayers for the Christian Year* (Grand Rapids, MI: William B. Eerdmans, 2007).

9. You can see a copy of the original diagram at Litsa Williams, "Grief Theory 101: The Dual Process Model of Grief," What's Your Grief? September 23, 2014, https://whatsyourgrief.com/dual -process-model-of-grief/.

Song List

I've selected these songs to accompany your daily readings because sometimes music speaks in ways that words never can. As you listen to these songs, allow the words, voices, and instruments to guide you into restful worship. It is an exquisite gift that, when we cannot sing for ourselves, the body of Christ sings with and for us. If you are struggling to trust God's promises, may this music rehearse those truths to your heart.

You can find these songs by searching on YouTube or another online service. You can also listen to them via my *Beyond the Darkness Devotional* Spotify playlist.*

- **Day 1:** *"Land of the Living (You Don't Lie)" by Church of the City*
- **Day 2:** *"How Long?" by The Porter's Gate*
- **Day 3:** *"Jesus Lover of My Soul" by Tasha Cobbs Leonard (featuring The Walls Group)*
- **Day 4:** *"Just a Closer Walk with Thee" by Patsy Cline*
- **Day 5:** *"Mourning into Dancing" by Steve Green*
- **Day 6:** *"The God Who Sees" by Kathie Lee Gifford and Nicole C. Mullen*
- **Day 7:** *"Holy Is the Lord" by Andrew Peterson*

---

* Go to Clarissa Moll, *Beyond the Darkness Devotional* playlist, Spotify, https://open.spotify .com/playlist/7hqCI2zss6Ya6CpgOzTfhC?si=56c31d8a88da4e55.

- *Day 8:* "Help My Unbelief" by Red Mountain Music
- *Day 9:* "God I Look to You" by Bethel Music
- *Day 10:* "Red Sea Road" by Ellie Holcomb
- *Day 11:* "Provision" by Mike Janzen
- *Day 12:* "I Glory in Christ" by Sandra McCracken
- *Day 13:* "No Vacant Thrones" by Phillip Joubert and Jonni Mae
- *Day 14:* "Yet Not I but through Christ in Me" by CityAlight
- *Day 15:* "Praise before My Breakthrough" by Bryan and Katie Torwalt
- *Day 16:* "I Am Thine, O Lord" by Grace Brumley
- *Day 17:* "You Love Me Best" by Ellie Holcomb
- *Day 18:* "Remembers Me (Psalm 105)" by Mike Janzen
- *Day 19:* "Let Me Find Thee" by Matthew Smith
- *Day 20:* "Come Thou Fount of Every Blessing" by Eclipse 6
- *Day 21:* "Not to Us" by Chris Tomlin
- *Day 22:* "You Know My Name" by Tasha Cobbs Leonard
- *Day 23:* "Your Labor Is Not in Vain" by The Porter's Gate
- *Day 24:* "Trust in You" by Lauren Daigle
- *Day 25:* "Surrounded (Fight My Battles)" by Michael W. Smith
- *Day 26:* "To Tell the Truth" by Sovereign Grace Music
- *Day 27:* "There's a Wideness in God's Mercy" by St. Paul's Cathedral Choir
- *Day 28:* "All through the Night" by Tom Roush
- *Day 29:* "Christ, Be Our Light" by Bernadette Farrell
- *Day 30:* "God Is Listening" by Gohar Almas
- *Day 31:* "Awake My Soul" by Chris Tomlin (featuring Lecrae)
- *Day 32:* "Your Plans for Us" by Eleventh Hour Worship
- *Day 33:* "Near the Cross" by The Petersens
- *Day 34:* "Those Who Have Not Seen" by Anchor Hymns
- *Day 35:* "Great Is Thy Faithfulness" by Austin Stone Worship
- *Day 36:* "If the Lord Builds the House" by Hope Darst
- *Day 37:* "There Was Jesus" by Zach Williams and Dolly Parton
- *Day 38:* "Abide" by Jonni Mae
- *Day 39:* "We Will Feast in the House of Zion" by Sandra McCracken
- *Day 40:* "Father, Let Your Kingdom Come" by The Porter's Gate

About the Author

Clarissa Moll is an award-winning writer and podcaster who helps bereaved people find flourishing after loss.

Clarissa's writing appears in *Christianity Today*, The Gospel Coalition, *RELEVANT*, Modern Loss, *Grief Digest*, and more. She cohosted *Christianity Today's Surprised by Grief* podcast and produces *Christianity Today's* flagship news podcast, *The Bulletin*. She holds a master's degree from Trinity Evangelical Divinity School and is a frequent guest on podcasts and radio shows.

Find her on Instagram at @mollclarissa or at clarissamoll.com.

Also from Clarissa Moll

Whether you've lost someone dear to you or you're supporting a loved one as they mourn, you can learn to walk with grief. In her debut book, Clarissa offers her powerful personal narrative as well as honest, practical wisdom that will gently guide you toward flourishing amid your own loss.

Available everywhere books are sold.